# KARMIC RELATIONSHIPS

Esoteric Studies

Vol. VII



RUDOLF STEINER

*Nine lectures given in Breslau between 7th and 15th June, 1924*

Translated by D. S. Osmond

RUDOLF STEINER PRESS

Rudolf Steiner Press
Hillside House, The Square
Forest Row, East Sussex
RH18 5ES

www.rudolfsteinerpress.com

First edition 1973
Reprinted 2002, 2009

Originally published in German as part of the title *Esoterische Betrachtungen karmischer Zusammenhänge, Fünfter Band* (volume 239 in the *Rudolf Steiner Gesamtausgabe* or Collected Works) by Rudolf Steiner Verlag, Dornach. This authorized translation published by permission of the Rudolf Steiner Nachlassverwaltung, Dornach



A catalogue record for this book is available from the British Library

ISBN 978 1 85584 218 2

Printed and bound in Great Britain by 4edge Limited

## SUMMARY OF CONTENTS

# EDITOR'S PREFACE

During the year 1924, before his illness in September, Rudolf Steiner gave over eighty lectures, published under the title *Karmic Relationships: Esoteric Studies*, to members of the Anthroposophical Society in the following places: Dornach, Berne, Zürich, Stuttgart, Prague, Paris, Breslau, Arnhem, Torquay and London. English translations of these lectures are contained in the following volumes of the series:

Vols. I to IV. Lectures given in Dornach (49).
Vol. V. Lectures given in Prague (4) and Paris (3).
Vol. VI. Lectures given in Berne (2) Zürich (1) Stuttgart (3) Arnhem (3).
Vol. VII. Lectures given in Breslau (9).
Vol. VIII. Lectures given in Torquay (3) and London (3).

All these lectures were given to members of the Anthroposophical Society only and were intended to be material for study by those already familiar with the fundamental principles of Anthroposophy. The following extract from the lecture of 22nd June, 1924 (see Vol. II) calls attention to the need for exactitude when passing on such contents:

"The study of problems connected with karma is by no means easy and the discussion of anything that has to do with the subject entails—or ought at any rate to entail—a sense of deep responsibility. Such study is in truth a matter of penetrating into the most profound mysteries of existence, for within the sphere of karma and the course it takes lie those processes which are the basis of the other phenomena of world-existence, even of the phenomena of nature... These difficult and weighty matters entail grave consideration of every word and every sentence spoken here, in order that *the limits within which the statements are made shall be absolutely clear...*"

The attention of readers is called to the fact that the fundamental explanations given by Rudolf Steiner of the laws and conditions of karma are contained in Vol. I of the series. Knowledge of the earlier lectures should therefore be regarded as an essential basis for study of those contained in the later volumes.

## *Lecture One*

It is by pointing to all-embracing secrets of cosmic existence that anthroposophical wisdom penetrates most deeply into the foundations of human life, for man is the microcosm in which all these secrets of the Universe are concentrated. The illumination coming from this vista of the Cosmos extends not only into the days but into the very hours of man's life in that it sheds light upon his karma, upon all the things that at every moment closely concern him. And so in these lectures I shall speak from many different angles of the anthroposophical basis of those ideas and conceptions which enable karma in human life to be more clearly recognised.

In man's earthly life between birth and death, two events or moments stand out clearly and distinctly from all others. One of them—it is not, of course, a 'moment' in the literal sense but you will understand what is meant—is the moment when as a being of spirit-and-soul, man comes down to earthly life, into a physical body which serves as an instrument for his activity on Earth. Not only does he clothe himself in this physical body but in it transforms his whole nature in order to become active on Earth. This is the moment, the event, of birth and conception—the beginning of earthly life. The other event is that of man's departure from earthly life, when he returns through the gate of death into the spiritual world.

Thinking, to begin with, of this latter event, we know that during the first hours and days after a man's death, the physical form remains preserved to a certain extent. But the question arises: How is this physical human form related to Nature, to the existence surrounding us in earthly life in the several kingdoms of Nature? Is the relation of these kingdoms of Nature, of external Nature as a whole to these remains of the human being such that they would be capable of preserving the structure intact? No, it is not. Nature is able only to *destroy* the physical form that has been built up since man's entry into earthly life; at death, the form which man regards as that of his earthly existence begins to disintegrate. Anyone who thinks deeply enough about this very obvious truth will realise that in the physical human form itself lies the refutation of the materialistic view. If the materialistic view were correct, it would have to be said that the human form is built up by Nature. But it is not so! Nature cannot build the human form, but only destroy it. This thought makes a very potent impression but one that is often quite wrongly formulated. It remains in the unconscious region of the soul, making itself strongly felt in everything we experience concerning the riddle of death. Now the express aim of Anthroposophy is to bring these riddles which life itself presents to any impartial mind, to the degree of solution necessary for the right conduct of life. Hence Anthroposophy must at the outset direct attention to the event of death.

On the other side there is the event of birth. Impartial self-observation is essential here if a picture comparable to that of death is to be obtained. This self-observation must be deeply concerned with the nature of human thinking. Thinking can be applied to everything that goes on in the physical world. We form our thoughts of what goes on in the world. If we did not do so we could not be men in the true sense for the power to form thoughts distinguishes us from all other beings around us in the realm of the Earth. But impartial observation of our thoughts makes them appear widely removed from the reality of existence around us. When we are engrossed in thought we become inwardly abstract, inwardly cold, in comparison with what we are in heart and soul when we surrender ourselves to life. No impartial mind will ever doubt that thoughts, as such, have a cold, abstract, arid quality. But clear insight into the life of thought should be one of the first meditative experiences of an anthroposophist. In contemplating this life of thought he will discern in it something very similar to the spectacle presented by a corpse. What is characteristic of the sight of a human corpse? As it lies there before us, we say to ourselves: A human soul and a human spirit once lived in this structure and have now departed from it. A corpse lies there as a husk of the soul and the spirit. But at the same time it provides us with proof that the world external to man could never have produced this particular structure, that it could have proceeded only from the soul and spirit, from the innermost core of man's nature, that it is the residue of something now no longer present. In its very form a corpse discloses that it is no truth *in itself* but only a remains of truth, having meaning only when soul and spirit are within it. In the form that remains a great deal has been lost but a corpse nevertheless shows that it was once the dwelling-place of soul and spirit.

If the eye of the soul is directed to the life of thought, this too, although from a rather different standpoint, will appear to have something corpse-like about it. Impartial observation of our own thinking reveals that in itself it can no more have real existence than the human form can have real existence in a corpse. In apprehending external Nature, there is as little intrinsic reality in human thinking as there is in a corpse. External Nature can certainly be apprehended by thoughts but can never herself produce them. For if Nature in herself were capable of producing thoughts there could be no such thing as logic which perceives, independently of all laws of Nature, what is sound or false in thinking. When we discern what a thought in the earthly world really is, it must appear to us as a corpse of the soul, just as what remains at the death of a human being appears as a physical corpse. The form of a corpse is comprehensible only when we see it as the remains left behind at death by a *living* man.—Imagine for a moment that there were on the Earth only a single human being, and that at his death a being belonging to the planet Mars were to come down and look at his corpse. It would be utterly incomprehensible to such a being. Were he to study all the forms in the mineral, plant and animal kingdoms he would find no explanation of how the form lying there dead could have come into existence. For this form is not only a contradiction in itself, it is a manifest contradiction of the whole extra-human, earthly world. Its very existence betrays that it has been abandoned by something; for by itself it could not exist.

So it is with our thoughts. If external Nature alone were responsible for producing them, they could never be as they are: they are a corpse of the soul, comparable with a physical corpse. The very existence of a corpse is evidence that something has died. What is it that has died in the case of thoughts? It is the kind of thinking that was ours before we came down into the earthly world. Abstract thinking is the corpse of what was once *living* thinking. The thinking of a soul as yet without a body is related to the form which thinking assumes in earthly existence as the human soul and spirit are related to the corpse. And we men in the physical body are the grave in which the pre-earthly, living life of the soul has been entombed. The thoughts were once alive in the soul; the soul has died to the spiritual world. We bear within us not the living thoughts but the corpse of the thoughts.

This is the picture presented by the spectacle of birth—the side of earthly life opposite to that of death. We speak more correctly than is usual in our time when we say: the spiritual in man dies through birth, the physical part of man dies through death.

If we find the approach to Anthroposophy through pondering on the phenomenon of death and so realising that our thinking is a corpse compared with pre-earthly thinking, our vista of man and of life on the Earth widens and we prepare in the right way to receive the teachings and the wisdom of Anthroposophy. The reason why it is so difficult for men to find the natural path to Anthroposophy is their erroneous conception of what is still present—although as a corpse—in earthly existence. To-day they place too high a value upon thinking but do not know what it really is: they know it only in its corpse-like character.

When we guide our thoughts in the direction I have been trying to indicate, the two sides of the eternal life of the human soul are brought into strong relief. In modern parlance there is only one word—a word fundamentally the offspring of human hopes—for the half of Eternity that begins now and has no end. We have only the word 'Immortality', because the question of what happens after death is of foremost importance to the men of our time. All their interests in life are bound up with knowing what happens after death. But there were epochs in the evolution of humanity when something else was of importance too. With his more egoistic thinking to-day a man says: 'What comes after death interests me because I should like to know whether my life will continue thereafter; what preceded birth or conception does not interest me.' He does not think about pre-earthly life as he does about the life after death. But the Eternity of the human soul has these two sides: Immortality and 'Unborn-ness'. Earlier Mystery-languages of men who under the conditions prevailing in their day still had vision of the supersensible world, had a word also for 'Unborn-ness', whereas we can formulate one only with difficulty, by deliberately turning our minds to these matters. Thereby we are also led to realise the essential difference between the laws of Nature and the laws governing human destiny.

Our human destiny seems, to begin with, to depend upon chance. Acting upon some urge or impulse, we achieve one thing or another and have to admit, in respect of ordinary life, that in innumerable cases the destiny of many a really good man brings him hard, painful and tragic experiences, whereas it will often happen that to one whose aims are far from good, life brings no hard but actually happy experiences.

With our ordinary, everyday consciousness we do not perceive the connection between what proceeds from our own soul and the destiny that befalls us. We see that the good may be followed by heavy blows of fate and that evil is not necessarily followed by anything except relatively favourable destiny. In the happenings of Nature we perceive how under the sway of necessity, effects follow causes, but in respect of the spiritual reality in which our normal life is contained this sway of necessity is not in evidence. Nevertheless an impartial survey of our life impels us to say: we ourselves have sought the stream of our destiny.

Let a man who has reached a certain age in this incarnation observe his earlier life quite objectively and impartially. He is, let us say, fifty years of age, and he surveys the course of the years back to childhood. He will then perceive how, following some inner urge, *he himself* made the approach to everything that befell him. It is not always a pleasant experience. But as he follows the events of his life backwards, he will be obliged to admit in respect of those that were really decisive that he made straight for those events in time, just as he may make straight for some point in space. The stream of destiny *issues from ourselves*. And so it is understandable when men such as Goethe's elderly friend Knebel say that observation of human life clearly reveals a plan running through it from beginning to end. True, this plan is not always such that in looking back over it a man will always insist that he would act in the same way again. But when he closely observes the details of his actions and their consequences, he will always perceive that an inner urge led from the earlier to the later. Thus are the various events in our lives explained. And this enables us to perceive that the law taking effect through our moral life of soul is entirely different from the law taking effect in the life of Nature. All this helps to create the attitude which should be adopted towards the spiritual investigator who from his vision of the spiritual world is as well able to describe the laws governing the forming of destiny as the naturalist is able to describe the laws of Nature. And to understand the working of spiritual law in the Universe is the task of Anthroposophy in our present age.

You will remember that in the book *Occult Science: an Outline* and elsewhere too, I have said that the Moon shining down upon us from the heavens was once united with the Earth, that at a certain point of time the physical Moon separated from the Earth and in a future age will again unite with it. Now it was not only the physical Moon that separated but with it went certain Beings who were on Earth when the physical Moon and the Earth were still one body. When we think of the spiritual treasures that have been contained in the evolution of humanity we shall be led inevitably to the conclusion that although in our present age men are exceedingly clever—and nearly all of them are—yet they are not truly wise. Treasures of wisdom, expressed not in an intellectual but in a more poetic, pictorial form, existed at the beginning of man's evolution on Earth, scattered through mankind by great Teachers, primeval Teachers who lived among men on Earth. These primeval Teachers were not incarnated in physical bodies, but only in etheric bodies and relations with them were different from relations between physical human beings. These Teachers moved about the Earth in etheric bodies and a man whose guide and leader they became felt in his soul their nearness to him. He felt something like an inspiration streaming into his soul; it was like an inner flashing up of truths, of visions too—for the teachings were imparted in a spiritual way. In that epoch of Earth evolution, beings were really of two categories: the visible and, for physical eyes, the invisible. Men did not clamour for sight of those beings who were not visible for they were able to receive their teachings without seeing them. Men heard the teachings rising up from within their souls and said to themselves: 'One of the great primeval Teachers of humanity has now drawn near to me.' No attempt was made to form any external pictures of these great Teachers. Men encountered them in spiritual experiences, they did not stretch out physical hands towards these Teachers, but encountered them nevertheless and felt something that was like a spiritual grasp of the hand.

It was these primeval Teachers who imparted to mankind the great treasures of wisdom of which only echoes have survived, even in creations such as the Vedas and the Vedanta philosophy. Even these great teachings of the East are no more than echoes. A primeval wisdom once spread among humanity on the Earth and then perished, in order that out of themselves, by their own volition, men might again be able to scale the heights to the spiritual world. Human freedom would not have been possible if the primeval Teachers had remained among men. Hence a comparatively short time after the Moon had separated from the Earth they followed in its wake, establishing their abode upon it. And there they have dwelt, supreme among the denizens of this Moon colony, ever since they separated from the Earth, leaving human beings to their own resources. Although we who pass from one earthly life to another no longer meet these great Teachers on Earth, we do so very shortly after passing through the gate of death. When the physical body has been laid aside at death, our etheric body expands and expands, but also becomes evanescent, and finally dissolves in the Universe. As soon as the etheric body has been laid aside a few days after death, we feel that our existence is no longer on the Earth but in the immediate environment of the Earth. When a few days have passed after death we feel that we are no longer living on the Earth; it is as though this terrestrial body has expanded as far as the sphere encircled by the orbit of the Moon. We feel that we are living on a magnified Earth; the Moon is no longer felt to be a separate body, but the whole sphere is felt as a unity, demarcated by the Moon's orbit; the Earth has expanded to become the Moon sphere, and has become spiritual. We are within the Moon sphere and there we remain for a considerable time after death. But to begin with we come together again with those spiritual Beings who at the beginning of man's existence on Earth were the great primeval Teachers. They are the first Beings whom we encounter in the Cosmos after our death; we eventually come again into their realm and there undergo a remarkable experience.

It might seem easy to picture existence after death—I shall still have to speak of its duration—as being shadowy in comparison with the life on Earth which gives the impression of being so robust. We can take hold of the things of earthly life; they, like physical men, are solid, compact; we say that something is real when we can actually take hold of it. But after death this robust earthly life seems like a dream, for entry into the Moon sphere brings us into an existence where everything seems to be much more real, much more saturated with reality than can ever be the case on Earth. This is because the great primeval Teachers of humanity who continue their existence in the Moon sphere permeate us with their own being, and enable everything to appear to us with greater reality than that which, as men of the Earth, we experience in the things of the world. And what is it that we experience in the Moon sphere?

Our experience of earthly life is, after all, fragmentary. Looking back over earthly life with ordinary consciousness, it appears to us as a single, continuous stream. But what has it been in reality? A day that has already become shadowy was followed by a night of which ordinary consciousness has no remembrance. Another day is followed by another night—and so it goes on. In memory we string together only the days but in a true retrospect the days must always be interrupted by what we have experienced during the nights. Ordinary consciousness fails here, and with a certain justification, because it is extinguished in sleep. When we are among these Moon Beings who were once the primeval Teachers of humanity, we live through precisely what we experienced during the nights here on the Earth. The length of time this form of existence in the Moon sphere lasts can therefore be computed. If a man is not an abnormally long sleeper he spends about one third of the duration of his earthly life in sleep. And life in the Moon sphere lasts for just so long, that is to say, for about one third of the duration of the life on Earth. A man who reaches the age of twenty spends about seven years in the Moon sphere; one who reaches the age of sixty, about twenty years, and so on. We live among these Beings and they permeate us with their form of existence.

But in order to understand life in this sphere we must think of what a man becomes when the physical body is laid aside. This is within the ken of an Initiate, and also of the dead. The moment a man has left the physical body behind at death, he is within the world that is *outside* that body. If as I stand here I were to go out of my body, I should first of all be within this table here, and then more and more deeply within everything around me in the world—only *not* inside my own skin. What was hitherto my inner world now becomes my outer world, and everything that was formerly my outer world becomes my inner world. My moral life too, becomes outer world. Suppose that I once gave another person a box on the ear in anger and my action made a grave moral impression upon him. Now I live backwards over my life to its fortieth year when I injured him in this way; in my life I may have laughed about the incident, but now I experience, not what *I* experienced at the time, but *his* physical pain, *his* moral suffering. With my whole being I am within him. In reality it was the same every night during sleep, but then it remained below the level of consciousness; it was a picture only, not an actual experience. After death, when we are permeated with the substance of the great primeval Teachers in the Moon sphere, the experience is infinitely more intense than it was on Earth. What on Earth is like a dream, is in yonder world a far stronger reality—and this is what we experience. This same intense reality is experienced, too, by one who with clairvoyant consciousness is able to follow a human being on his way after death and, through the attainment of Inspiration and super-sensible vision, to live with him as a real presence. Then we realise that the experiences through which men pass after death have far greater intensity and reality than the experiences undergone before death. And to experience what a human being is undergoing in his existence after death makes an incomparably stronger impression than earthly influences can ever make. To give you an example.—

Some of you will certainly be familiar with the figure of Strader in my Mystery Plays. The figure of Strader is drawn more or less from real life; such a personality existed and interested me profoundly. I followed the external life of this personality who is portrayed, with certain poetic modifications, in the figure of Strader. You know that I have written four Mystery Plays, in the last of which Strader dies. In 1913, when this fourth play was written, I could do no otherwise than let Strader die. And why? As long as the prototype of Strader was living in the physical world, my attention had been focused upon that prototype. But in the meantime this prototype had died. The whole man interested me so deeply that I continued to follow him, and the impressions coming from his life after death were so strong that they completely extinguished all interest in what he had been in his life on Earth. Not that the sympathy had waned, but it was simply not adequate after one had followed what he was experiencing after his physical death. In order to give these tremendously strong impressions some kind of poetic form, I was obliged to let Strader die, because his prototype had passed into the after-death existence—and the impressions coming from that were infinitely stronger than those of his earlier life on Earth.

This had practical consequences. One or two friends guessed who Strader's prototype had been in real life and with a certain noble devotedness set about investigating his literary estate. When with great delight they brought their findings to me, I was obliged, involuntarily, to be rather discourteous, because these findings did not interest me in the slightest. The strength of the impressions of the life after death effaced any interest in relics of the earthly life brought me by friends. And so indeed it is. These impressions, which are due to the fact that the Moon Beings imbue their very substance into man, drown everything that can be experienced in earthly life and infuse reality into existence. Hence, too, the compensatory deed is fraught with greater reality, since it results from experience of what a particular action signified to the one against whom it was directed. And our experience of what the other suffered is stronger than that caused in us by our own action.

Out of the experiences we undergo after death in the realm of the great primeval Teachers of humanity, the first seed of karma is formed. For there we resolve to make compensation for what we have done. Resolves, intentions, here take actual effect. On Earth the good does not always seem to be followed by good, nor evil by evil. But the resolves taken in a world of far greater reality than the earthly world, the experience that we ourselves must make compensation for what we have done—these resolves will lead in the later life to actual adjustment.

It is my intention to describe to you how karma gradually takes shape for a new life when, having lived through the time between death and rebirth, a man appears again in another incarnation. During the first period after death, through our communion with the Moon Beings, we form the resolve to fulfil our karma. I shall therefore try to give you a concrete picture of the stages by which in the life between death and a new birth, man's karma is formulated.

## *Lecture Two*

In the lecture yesterday we heard that man spends the first period of his life between death and a new birth in the Moon sphere, preparing the forces that will eventually take effect in his karma. In the Moon sphere he encounters Beings who were once together with him on the Earth as the great primeval Teachers of humanity. These are the Beings with whom he comes into contact almost immediately after death; he also comes into contact with the Hierarchy of Beings to whom the book *Occult Science: an Outline* refers as the Angeloi. The Angeloi have never been inhabitants of the Earth in the literal sense; they have never borne earthly bodies, nor even etheric bodies resembling those of men. The etheric bodies of the other Moon Beings of whom I spoke were not altogether dissimilar from those of men, but those Beings did not incarnate in physical bodies.

The Angeloi are the Beings who in the present period of our cosmic evolution guide us from one earthly life to another, and it is from the Moon sphere that they guide us. We have heard how in this same sphere the human being lays the foundations of his karma, gathers into himself the impulses which will bring about its ultimate fulfilment. But whatever has passed with a man through the gate of death as the result of unrighteous deeds, deeds which cannot be tolerated by the spiritual worlds—all this 'bad' karma, if I may so express it, must be left behind in the Moon sphere. For as he moves onwards through his life between death and a new birth, a man could not be encumbered with the consequences and effects of his unrighteous deeds. When he passes beyond the Moon sphere his inner life has expanded into a still wider region of the Cosmos, and he enters the Mercury sphere. Here he lives, primarily, in communion with the Beings belonging to the Hierarchy of the Archangeloi. In all these realms, of course, he is in contact with human souls who have also passed through the gate of death. In the Moon sphere, these are the third class of beings among whom he lives—they are disembodied human souls who, like himself, have passed through the gate of death. We shall presently see why the spiritual effects of the bad karma must remain behind in the Moon sphere. For the moment, the fact itself will suffice.

When man enters the Mercury sphere, he undergoes further purification. Even when he has laid aside in the Moon sphere those moral attributes which are unfit for the Cosmos, the spiritual counterparts of his physical weaknesses, of his physical infirmities, still remain with him, as do the tendencies to illness and the effects of the illnesses from which he suffered here on Earth. Surprising as it may seem, it is the case that in the life between death and a new birth, man lays aside his moral failings first and his physical infirmities only later, when he enters the Mercury sphere. In the Mercury sphere his soul is purged of the inner effects of those morbid processes which came to expression in illness during his life on Earth and in his soul he becomes completely healthy. You must remember that man is a single whole. From the occult standpoint it is erroneous to speak of him as a compound of spirit, soul and body. He is not a compound of these three constituents, but when we observe him he is revealed on the one side as body, on the other as spirit, and between body and spirit, as soul. In reality, man is one whole, a self-contained unity. The soul and the spirit too are involved in the conditions which prevail in illness. And when man has laid aside the physical body at death, the effects of the experiences resulting from the disease-processes are, to begin with, still present in his soul. But in the Mercury sphere these effects are obliterated under the influences of the Beings we know as the Archangeloi.

You see, therefore, that having passed stage by stage through the Moon sphere and the Mercury sphere, man becomes a being from whom moral and physical weaknesses have been removed. Then—after the lapse of many decades—

he enters the Venus sphere and there, as one who has lived through the spheres of Moon and Mercury, he is ready to pass from the Venus sphere into the Sun sphere where the longest period of life between death and a new birth is spent. The indications I am giving will show you how well-founded were the practices of those ancient Mysteries where men acted out of wisdom which, although it was an instinctive wisdom, was the outcome of wonderful powers of clairvoyance. In those olden times it would have been unthinkable to study medicine, for example, in the way that is customary nowadays. What happens now is that the purely physical symptoms of disease are observed and efforts are made to discover ameliorative measures by dissecting the corpse and observing the changes in evidence there, as compared with those which take place in the normal, living organism—and so forth. Such procedure would have been regarded as futile in the days of the ancient Mystery-wisdom when it was known that illumination leading to the healing of illness must come from the Beings of the Mercury sphere. For it was known that only if illumination proceeds from the whole nexus of cosmic processes can a man be healed fundamentally. The description of the Oracle of the Mercury Mysteries given from a different point of view in the book *Occult Science* indicates the nature of the practices in these Mysteries which were dedicated primarily to the ancient Art of Healing.

In the lecture yesterday we heard of the great primeval Teachers who were once together with men on Earth; wherever human beings dwelt, these Teachers were among them, peopling the etheric sphere of the Earth as a kind of second race. But in their dim, dreamlike consciousness men were aware that other Beings too came down among them, Beings whose abode has never been on the Earth. What has to be said about these things will of course seem not only paradoxical but sheer nonsense to the modern mind with its devotion to materialistic science. Nevertheless this 'nonsense' is the truth. The sages in the ancient Mysteries knew well that illumination on the processes of healing can be given only by the super-sensible Mercury Beings. And so through the sacred rites enacted in these Mysteries, spiritual Beings were able to come down from the Mercury sphere to the altars in the sanctuaries where the priests of the Mysteries conversed with them. The Beings who thus descended to the altars were known in the Mysteries simply as the *God Mercury*. The influence was the same, although it was not necessarily the same Being who descended on every occasion. Men's attitude to this sacred medicine in olden times was such that they said: the Art of Healing has been imparted by the God Mercury to his priest-healers.

Even to-day it cannot be said that Spiritual Science does not depend upon the help of Beings of the Cosmos who, when the necessary preparation has been made by Initiates, are able to come down to the Earth. Initiates of the Mystery-wisdom belonging to the modern age know well how much depends upon the possibility of conversing with Beings of the Cosmos. But the mentality prevailing to-day is utterly different from that of olden times. A doctor nowadays is one upon whom some University has conferred a medical degree, whereas in days of antiquity a doctor was one who had conversed with the God Mercury. But as time went on this converse took place no longer and only traditions remained of what was once achieved in the Mysteries when the priest-healers had conversed with the God.

In the Venus sphere it is a matter of leading over into the Sun sphere whatever still remains of the human being when his tendencies to unrighteousness and to illness have been eliminated. To understand this we must think of something that is characteristic of man. Here on Earth a man is always one whole, one undivided whole. Only if he is executed for some terrible crime is he no longer a single whole in respect of the physical body. However severe the punishment he may receive for lesser transgressions, he is still one whole. But this is not the case with the soul-and-spiritual counterpart which has passed through the Moon sphere and the Mercury sphere. When as a being still possessed of soul and spirit in the super-sensible world after death, man has cast off the weaknesses due to the wrongdoings and to illnesses, he is in a certain sense no longer whole. For a man is one with his wrongdoings; his sinfulness is part of him. If someone were so utterly villainous as to possess no good qualities at all, his whole being would have to remain in the Moon sphere and he could make no further progress; for to the extent to which we are evil, to that extent we leave our own being behind in the Moon sphere. We are one with, identical with, what is evil in us according to the standards of the spiritual world. Therefore when we arrive in the Venus sphere, we have been mutilated in a certain respect. In the Venus sphere the element of purest Love prevails—purest Love in the spiritual sense; and it is this Cosmic Love that bears what now remains of the human being from the Venus sphere into the Sun existence.

There, in the Sun existence, man has to work in a very real way at the moulding and shaping of his karma. Now if our physicists were ever to reach the Sun they would be astonished, to say the least of it! For everything that men claim to have discovered about the Sun is at variance with the facts. The Sun is supposed to be a kind of globe filled with incandescent gas—but that is far from the truth. Let us take a rather commonplace illustration. If you have some Seltzer water in a glass you will have to look carefully if you want to see the actual water, for what you see are the bubbles in the water. These bubbles are less dense than the water itself and you see what is the less dense. And now, what about the Sun? When you look at the Sun you do not see it because it is a globe of densified, incandescent gas in empty space, as science alleges, but you see it because just at that place there is a condition of utmost rarefication.—And now you must get accustomed to an idea that is far from familiar.-

You look out into space—I am not going to speak now about the nature of space. Here, when you look into the water, there are bubbles everywhere—bubbles which are thinner, less dense than the water. Where the Sun stands in the sky, conditions are less dense even than space. You will say: 'but space itself is void, it is nullity.' Nevertheless at the place where the Sun is situated there is actually *less* than nullity. It should not be difficult, especially in these days, for people to think of something else that is less than nothing. If there were originally five shillings in my pocket and I spend them one by one, in the end I have nothing. But when I get into debt I have less than nothing—which is the plight of a good many people to-day! Very well, then: where there is space, space alone, there is nothing; but where the Sun is there is *less* than nothing, there is a lacuna in space—and there dwell the spiritual Beings referred to in the book *Occult Science* as the Exousiai, the Dynamis, the Kyriotetes. There they have their abode, sending their own essence and power through all creation. Among them man spends the greater part of his life between death and a new birth. In association with the Exousiai, Dynamis, Kyriotetes, with human souls karmically connected with him who have also passed through the gate of death, and with yet other Beings whose existence is hardly even conjectured, the karma for the next earthly life is worked out and formulated. Conditions in this Sun region are not as they are on Earth. Why do our clever scientists—and clever they certainly are—picture the Sun as a globe of incandescent gas? It is because a certain illusory, materialistic instinct makes them want to detect physical processes in the Sun. But there is nothing physical in the Sun. One may at most speak of physical processes in the Sun's corona, but certainly not in the Sun itself. In the Sun there is nothing like natural law, for it is a world of purest spirit. Materialists would like to insist that the Sun too is under the sway of natural law, but it is not so. The only laws prevailing in the Sun are those which give effect to the karmic consequences of the Good and which operate in restoring the mutilation man has undergone as the result of his 'bad' karma when he has been transported by the Love of the Venus Beings into the Sun sphere. When the life of man between death and a new birth is described many will wonder how this very lengthy period is spent. Many things that happen on the Earth command admiration and awe, but the most sublime achievements of earthly civilisation are puny and insignificant in comparison with what is accomplished in a purely spiritual way during this Sun existence, when mighty Powers are all around and within us, working to the end that our karma shall take effect in the next earthly life.

The elaboration of part of man's karma is completed in the Venus sphere, and some part even in the Mercury sphere. Later on we shall hear of a certain well-known historical personality whose destiny in his incarnation in the nineteenth century was due to the fact that his karma was very largely wrought out in the spheres of Venus and Mercury. Souls who begin to give shape to their karma in these spheres often become personalities of outstanding significance in the subsequent incarnation. But in the great majority of cases the main part of the karma for the following earthly life is worked out in the Sun sphere, where the longest period is spent. We will speak in greater detail later on but to-day I will give an outline of how the foundations of karma are laid, stage by stage, in the various spheres. In order not to be confused by other descriptions I have given of the life between death and a new birth, you must be clear that in moving through these spheres man enters into entirely different conditions of cosmic existence. When the time comes for him to enter the Mars sphere, he is still not altogether outside the Sun sphere, for the influences of the Sun are still active in this part of the Cosmos which was once cast off by the Earth. In the Sun sphere, man is concerned only with his moral qualities and with those attributes of his being which have remained healthy; the rest has been laid aside. It persists in him as a kind of incompleteness but this is made good in the Sun sphere. During the first half of existence in the Sun sphere we are engaged in making preparation for the appropriate physical organisation of the next earthly body. During the second half of the Sun existence, in union with the Exousiai, Dynamis, Kyriotetes, and with human souls karmically connected with us, we are concerned with the preparation of the moral side of karma, the moral qualities which will then be present in the next life. But this moral part and the spiritual part of karma—for example, specific talents in one direction or another—are then further elaborated in the Mars sphere, in the Jupiter sphere and in the Saturn sphere. And in passing through these spheres we come to know what the 'physical' stars are in reality.

To speak of a 'physical' star is not really correct. For what is a star? Physicists imagine that combustion of gas or some process of the kind is taking place in the sky. But as I said, if they could actually get there they would be amazed to find no burning gas in the Sun but actually a lacuna, a gap in space, in a condition infinitely more rarefied than any particles of earthly matter could ever be. Everything is Spirit, pure Spirit. Nor are the other stars so many bodies of incandescent, burning gas, but something entirely different. Bordering on this Earth with its physical substances and physical forces, is the universal Cosmic Ether. We are able to perceive the Cosmic Ether because, as we gaze into it, our field of vision is circumscribed and the surrounding ether appears blue. But to believe as materialistic thinkers do, that physical substances are roaming around up there in the Cosmos is just childish fancy. No physical substances are moving around, for at the place where a star is seen, there is something altogether different. The farthest reaches of the etheric would lead out of and beyond space, into the spheres where the Gods have their abode. And now picture to yourselves a certain inner relationship which may exist between one person and another and comes to physical expression. Picture it quite graphically. You are caressed by someone who loves you. You feel the caress but it would be childish to associate it in any way with physical matter. The caress is not matter at all, it is a process, and you experience it inwardly, in your *soul.* So it is when we look outwards into the spheres of the Ether. The Gods in their love caress the world. But the caress lasts long, because the life of the Gods spans immense reaches of time. In very truth the stars are the expression of love in the Cosmic Ether; there is nothing physical about them. And from the cosmic aspect, to see a star means to feel a caress that has been prompted by love. To gaze at the stars is to become aware of the love proceeding from the divine-spiritual Beings. What we must learn to realise is that the stars are only the signs and tokens of the presence of the Gods in the Universe. Physical science has much to learn on its path from illusion to truth! But men will not achieve self-knowledge nor will they understand their own true being until this physical science has been transformed into a spiritual science of the worlds beyond the Earth. Science in its present form has meaning only for the Earth, for physical matter in the real sense* exists only on the Earth. And so when we depart from the Earth at death, we enter more and more into a life of purely spiritual experiences. The reason why our physical life presents an entirely different aspect in these backward-streaming experiences which continue for a third of the length of earthly existence, is that we have been permeated with the essence and substance of the Moon sphere. The preparation of karma is one of the many things that have to be accomplished in the worlds of the stars.

In order that one set of facts may be supported by others, let me explain how such observations are made by one who is versed in modern Initiation Science. For some time now, even in public lectures, I have been describing how when a man develops the faculty of genuine supersensible perception through the methods indicated in the book, *Knowledge of the Higher Worlds*, he looks back over his earthly life, seeing it as a kind of tableau. Everything is present *simultaneously*, in a mighty panorama of the whole of life since the birth of the 'I'; but the several epochs are in a certain respect distinct from each other. We survey our experiences from birth until the change of teeth, then again, as one complete series, the experiences occurring between the time of the change of teeth and puberty, then the experiences of the period from puberty until the beginning of the twenties, and so forth. Further concentration and application of the methods for the attainment of spiritual knowledge enable

* The difference between *physical* and *mineral* matter must be remembered here.

us, as we survey this tableau, to observe, firstly, our life from birth to the seventh year. But later on these pictures are allowed to fade away and we see right *through* our life; when the consciousness has been emptied of all pictorial impressions and we have achieved Inspiration, we behold the living, weaving activity of the Moon sphere in place of the tableau of early childhood from birth until the seventh year. We behold this living, weaving activity. And so Initiation in the form that is normal and right for this present age brings us knowledge of the secrets of the Moon sphere, when the pictures of our own life up to the seventh year are obliterated in the consciousness of Inspiration and we perceive what now flashes up in their place.

Then, if we observe the tableau of life between the seventh and fourteenth years and again obliterate the pictures in the consciousness of Inspiration, we gaze into the Mercury sphere. Everything has to do with the being of man, for man is an integral part of the whole Universe. If he learns to know himself as he really is, in the innermost core of his being, he learns to know the whole Universe. And now I would ask you to pay attention to the following.—Deepest respect arises in us for the old, instinctive Initiation Science which gave things that have remained in existence to this day, their true and proper names. Designations that are coined nowadays result in nothing but confusion, for modern scholarship is incapable of naming things in accordance with reality. An unprejudiced observation of life will fill us with reverence for the achievements of ancient Initiation Science. Ancient Initiation Science knew by instinct something that is confirmed to-day by statistics, namely, that the illnesses of childhood occur most frequently in the *first* period of life; it is then that the human being is most prone to illness, and even to death; after puberty this tendency abates, but the healthiest period of all, the period when mortality is at its lowest, is between the ages of seven and fourteen. The wise men of old knew that this is due to the influences of the Mercury sphere and again to-day we may make the same discovery when through modern Initiation Science we penetrate the secrets of existence. Such things fill us with reverence for these sacred traditions of humanity.

By looking back into our experiences from the fourteenth to the twenty-first years and obliterating the pictures in the consciousness of Inspiration, we are led to the secrets of the Venus sphere. Here again the wonderful wisdom of ancient Initiation Science comes into evidence. The human being reaches puberty; love is born. When the pictures of this period of life are illumined by Initiation Science, the secrets of the Venus sphere are disclosed. Everything I am now describing is part of the true self-knowledge which unfolds in this way.

When the pictures of experiences occurring between the twenty-first and forty-second years of life are eliminated in the consciousness of Inspiration, we are led to the Sun sphere. Through deepened self-knowledge the secrets of the Sun sphere can be experienced in this retrospective contemplation of the events of our life between the twenty-first and forty-second years. To acquire knowledge of the Sun existence our vision must cover a period three times longer than that of the periods connected with the other planetary bodies.

I told you that the karma of a certain well-known personality in history had taken shape paramountly in the spheres of Mercury and Venus, and you will now understand how such things are investigated. We look back, firstly, into the period of our own life between the seventh and fourteenth years, and then into the period between the fourteenth and twenty-first years; when the pictures have been eliminated in the consciousness of Inspiration, light is shed upon the secrets of the Mercury sphere and the Venus sphere. Through this illumination we perceive how such an individuality worked together with the Beings of the higher Hierarchies and with other human souls, and how his subsequent earthly incarnation in the nineteenth century took shape.

Now if the elaboration of karma has taken place mainly in the *Mars* sphere, investigation is more difficult. For if a man attains Initiation before the age of 49, it is not possible for him to look back into the period of life which here comes into question, namely, the period between the forty-second and forty-ninth years. He must have passed his forty-ninth year if he is to be able to eliminate the pictures of this particular set of experiences and penetrate the secrets of the Mars sphere. If Initiation is attained after the age of fifty-six it is possible to look back into the period between the forty-ninth and fifty-sixth years of life, when karma that is connected with the *Jupiter* sphere takes shape. And now we are at the point where the various sets of events come together in one connected whole.

It is not until the period between the fifty-sixth and sixty-third years can be included in this retrospective vision that we are able to survey the whole range of experiences and to speak out of our own inner knowledge. For then we can gaze into the profoundly significant secrets of the *Saturn* sphere. Karmas that were wrought out mainly in the Saturn sphere operate in mysterious ways to bring men together again in the world. In order to perceive all these connections in the light of Initiation Science itself—they can of course be explained and so become intelligible—but in order to perceive with independent vision and be able to judge them, we must ourselves have reached the age of sixty-three. A human being appears in some earthly life—thus for example there is a certain great poet of whom I shall speak later—and we find that through his faculties, through his literary creations, he was giving expression to that in his karma which could have been wrought out only in the Saturn sphere.

When we look up to the Sun, to the planetary system—and the same applies to the rest of the starry heavens for they are connected in a very real way with the being of man—we can witness how human karma takes shape in the Cosmos. The Moon, the planets Venus, Jupiter—verily these heavenly bodies are not as physical astronomy describes them. In their constellations, in their mutual relationships, in their radiance, in their whole existence, they are the builders and shapers of human destinies, they are the cosmic timepiece according to which we live out our karma. As they shine downwards from the heavens their influences have real power. This was known in the days of the ancient Mystery-wisdom but the old Astrology—which was a purely *spiritual* science, concerned with the spiritual foundations of existence—has come down to posterity in a degraded, amateurish form. Anthroposophy alone can contribute something that will enable us to perceive the spiritual connections as they truly are and to understand how through the great timepiece of destiny, human life on Earth is shaped according to law.

From this point of view let us think of the human being and his karma. Those who with the help of Anthroposophy evolve a healthy conception of the world as against the unsound views prevailing to-day, will unfold not only quite different concepts and ideas but also quite different feelings and perceptions. For you see, if we really understand the destiny of a man, we also learn to understand the secrets of the world of stars, the secrets of the Cosmos. But nowadays people write biographies without the faintest inkling that something is really being profaned by the way in which they write. In times when knowledge was held to be sacred because it issued from the Mysteries, nobody would have written biographies in the way that is customary to-day. Every ancient 'biography' contained indications of the influences and secrets of the world of stars. In human destiny we can perceive, firstly, the working of the Angeloi, Archangeloi, Archai; then of still loftier Sun Beings, Exousiai, Dynamis, Kyriotetes; then of the Thrones who are concerned mainly with the elaboration of karma in the Mars sphere; then of the Cherubim who elaborate the karma belonging to the Jupiter sphere; and then of the Seraphim who work together with man at the elaboration of karma in the Saturn sphere—Saturn karma. In a man's destiny, in his karma, we behold the working of the higher Hierarchies. This karma, at first, is like a veil, a curtain. If we look behind this veil we gaze at the weaving deeds and influences of Angeloi, Archangeloi, Archai, Exousiai, Dynamis, Kyriotetes, Thrones, Cherubim, Seraphim. Every human destiny is like script on a sheet of paper. Just imagine that someone looking at the writing on the paper were to say that he can see signs - K - E - I, and so forth, but he is quite unable to combine these letters into words! As there are some twenty-two to twenty-eight letters (to be exact, about thirty to thirty-four in all) such a man could only conceive that the whole of Goethe's *Faust* is made up entirely of those thirty-four letters. He cannot read, therefore he sees only the different letters. When someone else finds a great deal more in *Faust* because he can combine the letters into the words of which this wonderful work is composed, an out-and-out illiterate with no notion of how to read may say with horror: Here is someone who actually thinks that all kinds of things are contained in *Faust*—but he is an utter fool! Yet the whole of *Faust* does actually consists of these letters. Similarly, when we observe the karma of a human being in the ordinary way, we see letters only; but the moment we begin to *read* this karma we behold the Angeloi, Archangeloi, Archai and their mutual, interrelated deeds. The destiny of an individual human life becomes the richer, the more we get beyond the thirty-four letters and find in them—*Faust*! And the picture of a human destiny is enriched beyond measure when earthly ignorance is transformed into knowledge of the Cosmic Alphabet, when we realise that the letters of that script are the signs and tokens of the deeds of the Beings of the higher Hierarchies.

To a man who beholds it, the vista of karma as the shape taken by destiny in life is so overwhelming, so sublime and majestic that simply by understanding how karma is related to the spiritual Cosmos he will unfold quite different qualities of feeling and discernment. It will not remain so much theoretical knowledge. What we acquire through Anthroposophy should not be a mere accumulation of theoretical information but should work more and more upon our life of thought and feeling, in that it rids us of the notion that we live an earthworm's existence and makes us aware that we belong to the land of Spirits. Verily, we are citizens not of the Earth alone but of the land of Spirits. The whole existence we have spent between death and a new birth converges in that which, on Earth, is enclosed within our skin. The secrets of worlds are contained in a particular form within this encircling skin.

Self-knowledge is by no means the trivial sentimentality of which there is so much talk nowadays. Human self-knowledge is world-knowledge. And so when friends have given me an opportunity, I have often written down for them the following lines:

If thou would'st know thy Self,
Look out into the Cosmic Spaces.
If thou would'st fathom the Cosmic Spaces,
Look inwards, into thine own Self.

*Willst Du Dein Selbst erkennen,*
*Schaue hinaus in die Weltenweiten.*
*Willst Du die Weltenweiten durchschauen,*
*Blicke hinein in das eigene Selbst.*

## *Lecture Three*

The conception of karma and its background given in the lecture yesterday can be deepened in many essential respects. We heard that behind human destiny there are worlds in relation to which the aspect of destiny usually observed amounts to no more than the letters of a script as compared with what is produced by the combinations of those letters in a work such as Goethe's *Faust*. Behind the destiny of a human being we can in very truth gaze at the life and weaving deeds of higher worlds and of the Beings belonging to those worlds. But this picture can be deepened and elaborated.—When man is passing through the Moon sphere after death, he lives in communion with the great primeval Teachers of humanity who have their abode in that sphere. Through the whole of the period between death and a new birth he is associated with human souls—particularly those with whom he is karmically connected—who have also passed through the gate of death and are living through the same period of spiritual existence. In the Moon sphere man lives in communion with the Beings we know as the Angeloi, Archangeloi and Archai, and as he passes through the following planetary spheres, with higher and ever higher Beings. It is not really correct to make demarcations and assign one particular Hierarchy to each heavenly sphere, for this is not in accord with reality. But in a general sense it can be said that the Archai, Archangeloi and Angeloi enter into communion with us before we pass into the Sun sphere; in that sphere we find our way into what has to be accomplished between death and a new birth in cooperation with the Hierarchy of the Exousiai, Dynamis, Kyriotetes. And then we gradually live on into the realms of the Thrones, Cherubim and Seraphim as we approach the Mars sphere and the Jupiter sphere. It is not correct to say that one Hierarchy corresponds only to one particular planetary sphere; but there is something else that will have important bearings when we come to study karmic relationships in greater detail.

It will, however, be necessary to familiarise ourselves with a conception which, to begin with, will seem strange and perplexing to ordinary thinking. As we stand on the Earth and feel our way into existence, we conceive of the Earthly as being immediately around us, on, under, and a little above the surface of the Earth in the environment, and when our minds turn to the so-called super-Earthly, our gaze is instinctively directed upwards. We feel the super-Earthly to be above us. Strange as it seems, it is true nevertheless, that when we ourselves are within those super-Earthly realms to which we look upwards from the Earth, when we are actually within them, the opposite holds good; for then we look *downwards* to the Earthly—which now lies below. In a certain sense we do so through the whole of our existence between death and a new birth. The question will occur to you: Is our experience of earthly things during physical existence so inadequate that between death and rebirth we have to look down from those super-earthly spheres to the Earth as a kind of nether heaven below us? . . . . But something else must be remembered here. The vista of all that we behold around us and in the cosmic expanse while we live on Earth between birth and death in a physical body enclosed by the skin, this vista is majestic and splendid; it refreshes and delights us, or it may bring tragedy and pain. At any rate it is a vista of rich and abundant life and a man might well believe that in comparison with the majesty of the world of stars, with everything that is revealed to him as his outer world, what is enclosed within his skin during physical existence is puny and insignificant. But the vista before us in our life between death and a new birth is entirely different. All that was our outer world during life on Earth now becomes our inner world. We feel ourselves expanding ever more and more into the cosmic spheres. What is there experienced may be described in earthly language in somewhat the following way.

Here on Earth we say, 'my heart'—meaning something that is inside our skin. Between death and a new birth we do not say, 'my heart', but 'my Sun'. For at a certain stage between death and rebirth, when our being has expanded into the Universe, the Sun is within us just as here on Earth the heart is within us—and the same applies in a spiritual sense to the rest of the starry worlds as I have described. Conversely, what was enclosed within our skin on Earth now becomes our outer world. But do not imagine that it bears any resemblance to what an anatomist sees when he dissects a corpse. The spectacle is even grander and more majestic than the panorama of the Universe presented to us on Earth. From the vantage-point of our life between death and a new birth, a whole world is revealed in what the physical senses perceive merely as heart, lung, liver, and so forth; it is a world greater and more impressive than the outer Universe at which we gaze during life on Earth.

Another singular fact is the following.—You may say: 'Yes, but as this world is present in every human being, everyone who dies must carry a separate world within him through death, and this suggests that the worlds to be perceived in the after-death existence greatly outnumber the individuals with whom one actually comes in contact there . . .' The secret lies in the fact that, firstly, all those human beings with whom we have some karmic tie are seen as a unity, as one world. Then there are the other souls who also form a unified, though less defined whole: this host of souls is linked with those with whom we have actual karmic ties, and again there is a unified whole. The moment we pass from the physical world into the spiritual world, everything is different. A great deal that has to be said will seem paradoxical to those unaccustomed to such conceptions but it is necessary now and again to draw attention to the conditions prevailing in the spiritual world as revealed to Initiation-wisdom. In the physical world we can count: one, two, three . . . we can also count money—although perhaps not just at the present time!—but counting does not really mean anything in the spiritual world. Number has no particular significance there; everything is more or less a unity. If things are to be counted they must be distinct and separate from each other and this does not apply in the spiritual world. In describing the spiritual world and the physical world, quite different terms have to be used in each case. From the vantage-point of the spiritual world, that which in the physical world is *within* man, presents a very different appearance. Man's structure is even more splendid, more awe-inspiring than the structure of the Heavens as perceived from the Earth. And what we prepare in communion with the higher Hierarchies for the incarnation that will follow the life between death and a new birth must be an entelechy of soul-and-spirit that befits this human structure, permeates it, gives it life.

How does the life of a human being develop on Earth? When we are born from pre-earthly existence into earthly life, the whole physical body has, apparently, been provided by our parents. It may seem as though having come down from the supersensible world we unite in a purely external way with what has been prepared for us in the physical world by our parents and has developed in the mother's body. What happens in reality, however, is the following.—

The substance of the physical body is constantly changing; it is all the time being thrown off and replaced. Think only of your finger-nails and your hair. You cut your finger-nails and they grow again. But this is only a process that is externally perceptible; in reality, man is all the time throwing off matter and replacing it from within, from the inner centre of his being. Substance is perpetually scaling off and in seven or eight years time all the physical substance that was within us seven years previously has been thrown off and replaced by new. Just think of this.—Seven years ago I was able, to my great joy, to lecture to friends here in Breslau. There they were, sitting on chairs in front of me; but nothing remains to-day of the physical substance contained in those bodies; it has all vanished and been replaced by other physical substance. What has remained in each case is the individuality of spirit-and-soul. The individuality was present before birth, in pre-earthly existence, in earlier earthly lives too, and has remained. But the substance of the bodies sitting in the chairs seven years ago has long since passed away into other regions of the Universe. Now this exchange of substance begins at birth and is complete after the lapse of seven years or so. What our parents provide is the substance and its particular organisation up to the time of the change of teeth. Thereafter the task of moulding the substance is taken over by the individuality. The change of teeth is a process of great significance. Until that time we have received from our parents a *model*; this model resembles our parents, embodies the hereditary traits. Then, in accordance with this model, the individuality of spirit-and-soul slowly builds up the second body which exists from the time of the change of teeth to the onset of puberty, is then cast off, and the third body begins to develop. Hereditary traits which remain in us are due to the fact that in the second body we have copied them from the model. What is copied from the model at a later stage is adapted and elaborated by the unconscious faculty, acquired in pre-earthly existence, to mould the human organism in accordance with the secrets it contains. The purpose of the first body which we bear until the time of the change of teeth is to enable us, in conformity with our karma, to resemble our parents. The real secrets, the deep, all-embracing secrets whereby the human organism is built up as the wonderful image of the outer structure of the Heavens—these secrets in their innermost essence have to be acquired during the life between death and a new birth.

Having lived through the first half of the Sun-existence we have to find our way into the second half, where the impulse to live out our karma is kindled. Here again a vista lies before us of wonderful happenings which take place between ourselves and the Beings of the higher Hierarchies.

Here on Earth we live and move among minerals, plants, animals, other human beings; between death and a new birth we live together with other human souls in the way described—but now, instead of minerals, plants, animals, there are the Archai, Archangeloi, Angeloi, and together with them we shape our karma. Through the whole of the time we gaze at the earthly realm below where our karma must take effect, gaze at it longingly, as something to which all our forces of feeling are directed,—just as here on Earth between birth and death we gaze upwards with longing to the Heavens. In ascending to the Moon sphere, Mercury sphere, Venus sphere, we find our way to the Beings of the Hierarchy of Archai, Archangeloi and Angeloi. These Beings are the judges of what is good and evil in us, also of the mutilation we undergo, as I described in the previous lecture. For the consequence of unrighteousness is that we suffer a kind of mutilation as beings of soul and spirit. There, in these higher spheres, we have our judges, we are involved in the operations of Cosmic Justice.—In the Sun-existence we reach the sphere of the Exousiai, Dynamis, Kyriotetes. We are now within the ranks of Beings who do not only judge but actually work with us at the shaping of our karma. These Beings—Exousiai, Dynamis, Kyriotetes—are primarily denizens of the Sun, and therewith of the whole Universe. They belong essentially to spiritual worlds. But mediators are necessary between the spiritual world and the material, physical world, and these mediators are the Thrones, Cherubim and Seraphim. Their rank in the spiritual Cosmos is higher because they are mightier Beings—mightier not merely in the realm of spiritual life but because they bring to effect in the physical world what is thus lived through in the spiritual worlds. In the life between death and a new birth we gaze consciously and with longing at the earthly realm below, but in reality we are gazing at what is proceeding among the Seraphim, Cherubim and Thrones, in their mutual connections with one another. It is a shattering, awe-inspiring experience. We learn, gradually, to understand the deeds performed between Seraphim and Seraphim, Cherubim and Cherubim, Thrones and Thrones, and again between Thrones and Seraphim, Thrones and Cherubim, and so forth. These Beings are engaged in bringing about a process of adjustment which, as we learn to understand it, we feel has something to do with ourselves. What is it, in reality? It is the image that arises in cosmic existence from the good and the evil for which we were responsible in our earthly life. The good must result in good; the evil must result in evil. Seraphim, Cherubim and Thrones elaborate the consequences of what we have sown on Earth; our evil deeds have injurious consequences in cosmic existence. We witness how Seraphim, Cherubim and Thrones are occupied with the consequences of our evil deeds. And the knowledge gradually dawns upon us that in what comes to pass in cosmic evolution among the Seraphim, Cherubim and Thrones, our karma is being lived out in the Heavens before we can live it out on Earth. This awe-inspiring experience is enhanced inasmuch as we now realise with all the force we possess in this spiritual life between death and a new birth, that what the Seraphim, Cherubim and Thrones experience in their divine existence finds its just fulfilment when we ourselves experience it in the next earthly life. Thus in super-earthly realms our karma is lived through in advance by the Seraphim, Cherubim and Thrones. In very truth the Gods are the Creators of the Earthly. They live through everything in advance, in the realm of spirit; then in the physical realm it comes to fulfilment. Our karma is prefigured by the Seraphim, Cherubim and Thrones in their divine existence. Thus are the forces which shape our karma set in operation.

During existence in the planetary spheres we experience the deeds, the judgements, of the Archai, Archangeloi, Angeloi. But Seraphim, Cherubim and Thrones are also at work, in order that they may live through our karma in advance. Thus are we made aware of the debt we owe to the world on account of our previous deeds, thus do we experience the divine foreshadowing of what our life is to be. These experiences are complex and intricate, but they are part and parcel of that super-earthly existence upon which earthly life is based.

Not until we realise how rich in content is the life between death and a new birth and think of this in conjunction with the happenings of earthly life do we obtain a really adequate conception of what comes to pass in the world through man and in man. Thus is self-knowledge deepened, enriched and spiritualised. The only way whereby we can obtain a true picture of the earthly life of humanity is to view it against the background of happenings in the spiritual world.

We see human beings appearing on the Earth; they are born, grow up, are creative or active according to their destiny and the particular faculties they possesss. The historical life of humanity through the ages is, after all, the outcome of human faculties, human deeds, human thoughts and feelings. But all these human beings who appear in an earthly life between birth and death—all of them have passed through previous lives in which they experienced the Earthly in a different way, worked upon it in a different way. The influences of earlier lives make themselves felt in all later lives, but it is only possible to understand the sequence of connections by taking account, too, of the periods lying between death and rebirth. Then, for the first time, we have a true conception of history, for we realise that what appears on the Earth through human beings in one epoch is linked with the happenings of an earlier epoch. But the essential question is: How are the fruits and happenings of an earlier epoch carried over into later times?—Historians have long been content to record consecutive facts but from data of this kind it is impossible to understand *why* later events follow those that preceded them. Some have said that ideas are at work in history and then become actuality. But no genuine thinker can conceive why this should be so. Others—those who hold the materialistic view of history—say: Ideas—so much twaddle! Economic factors are the only reality, they lie at the root of everything!—Such is the materialistic, mechanistic conception of history.

But this is no more than a dabbling on the surface of things. The reality is that what came to pass in earlier epochs of history is carried over into later epochs *by human beings themselves*. All those who are sitting here now lived in earlier epochs. Their deeds and manner of acting are the consequences of what they experienced in earlier lives. And so it is with everything that comes to pass in the course of history, be it of importance or of little account. The earlier is carried over into the later by human souls themselves. The conception of life prevailing nowadays can be deepened in the true sense only by the realisation that historical evolution too is borne onwards by man himself. But everything is determined by what is achieved in the starry worlds between death and rebirth where man works in cooperation with the Beings of the higher Hierarchies.

And now let us take an example to illustrate what has been said. In comparatively early times, not long before the founding of Christianity, a certain Initiate was incarnated in the East, in the Indian civilisation. In his earthly life this individuality had poor eyesight—in describing karmic relationships one must go into details of this kind—and his perceptions remained more or less superficial. This life which was characterised by the mystical outlook typical of Indian culture, was followed by other, less important incarnations. But there was a life between death and a new birth during which the superficial experiences of the Indian incarnation were worked upon in the Mercury sphere, partly too in the Venus sphere and in the Mars sphere, in conjunction with Beings of the higher Hierarchies. In the majority of human beings the influences of *one* of the cosmic spheres are dominant in the shaping of the karma, but in the case of this particular individuality the influences of the Mercury sphere, the Venus sphere and the Mars sphere worked with almost equal strength at the karmic transformation of incipient faculties arising from the experiences of an Indian incarnation. In the nineteenth century this individuality appeared again as a somewhat complex personality, namely, *Heinrich Heine.*

Let us think about an example such as this which has been brought to light from the depths of spiritual life by very penetrating and exact investigation. A rigid, superficial thinker will argue that this tends to take away the whole atmosphere and quality of the personality, that what he wants is a picture of the elementary characteristics of the man in question . . . well, he has every right to take this attitude if he chooses; it is his karma to be a philistine and he has the right to speak in this way . . . but he will not succeed in reaching more than a fragment of the truth. When we look more deeply into the facts, the foundations and the background of the reality come to light. The life of an individual is certainly not impoverished but infinitely enriched in meaning when it is studied in the light of such foundations, when we can perceive the experiences of an earlier, Indian incarnation glimmering through that problematic, fitful Heine-life. Having absorbed the influences operating in the Mercury sphere and the Venus sphere, this individuality passed into the Mars sphere, where a certain strain of aggressiveness developed for the next earthly life; the experiences of an earlier life were transformed into a faculty in which there was a certain vein of aggressiveness. In the Mercury sphere the soul acquired the tendency to flit from one experience to another, one concept to another, and in the Venus sphere an element of eroticism—eroticism in the spiritual sense—crept into the imaginative, conceptual faculties.

In surveying a human life in this way we gaze into cosmic existence, and what we thus perceive is certainly not poorer in content than the commonplace picture of a man's elementary characteristics desired by superficial observers. We perceive how earlier history is carried over into later history through the instrumentality of the starry worlds and the Beings of those worlds. History becomes reality only when it is viewed in this setting; otherwise it remains so many disjointed ciphers. But now we begin to read from history how behind the individual destinies of men there are the deeds of Gods and of worlds which become manifest in ever greater grandeur and power in the process of the historical evolution of humanity—where we shall always discern the weaving of the destinies and the thoughts of individuals.

And now, another example.—There is an individuality who at the time when Islam was spreading across North

Africa to Spain, had acquired much scholarship according to the standards then prevailing. Schools similar to that in which St. Augustine had received instruction still existed in North Africa, but now, in a later period, the School had fallen into decline. This individuality imbibed a great deal of the knowledge that had been preserved in these Schools in which much wisdom deriving from the ancient Mysteries still survived, although in a decadent form. Then his path took him to Spain where he came in contact with the earlier —not the later—Cabbalistic School, acquired much of this earlier Cabbalistic learning and thus became thoroughly versed in Manichean-Cabbalistic doctrine. In the course of further development during a life between death and a new birth, a certain strain of aggressiveness was acquired and, in addition, a talent which had something rather dangerously fascinating about it, namely, fluency of speech and language in dealing with all kinds of problems which arose in the soul from the earlier incarnation. With these characteristics the individuality in question was born again in the eighteenth century as *Voltaire*.

To know that the Voltaire-life leads back to experiences akin to those of St. Augustine in his early days, experiences which were associated with the Cabbalistic School and hence with all the irony peculiar to Cabbalistic learning, to know that all these elements play a part and, by penetrating into what happened during life between death and rebirth, to perceive the connection between the two lives—this alone can lead to a picture of the whole reality. At first sight there seems to be no connection between successive earthly lives; we do not perceive how the one reaches over into the other. The intervening periods are not perceived but for all that they are fragments of the whole picture in which everything is embraced. It is only by studying the spiritual background as well as the earthly nature of a man that we can hope to approach reality.

In this connection a new trend must take effect on our Movement, from now onwards. When the German Section of the Theosophical Society was founded in Berlin in 1902,

I gave as the title of my first lecture: *Studies of the concrete working of Karma.* The lecture was announced but could not be delivered for the simple reason that the older members of the Theosophical Society had their own ideas of what may or may not be spoken about, and this attitude had determined the whole atmosphere. The leading Members would have been horrified if at that time one had spoken of the concrete workings of karma. The Theosophical Movement was not ready for it. A great deal of preparation was necessary and has, in fact, been going on now for more than two decades. But at the Christmas Foundation Meeting the impulse was given to speak without reserve, not only about the Spiritual in general but also about what can be discovered concerning man's life in the realm of spirit. And so in future we shall speak quite openly in the Anthroposophical Society of matters of which from the very beginning it was the intention to speak, but for which preparation had to be made. This is part of the esoteric trend and impulse with which the Anthroposophical Society was imbued through the Christmas Foundation Meeting. The Christmas Meeting was no trifling episode; it betokened the assumption of new responsibilities for the Anthroposophical Movement, responsibilities flowing from the realm of spirit.

To be able to gaze at what takes place between death and a new birth brings home to one the rich diversity and many-sidedness of the world. For when it is said that the qualities of aggressiveness and also of fluency of language are quickened in the Mars sphere, this is only one aspect; other aspects of life too are quickened in that sphere. And the same applies to the Jupiter sphere. The Jupiter sphere and its Beings are experienced when in the process of self-observation one looks back with the insight of Initiation over the period between the forty-ninth and fifty-sixth years of life—and then obliterates the pictures. The vista of the Jupiter sphere may be a shattering experience, for the Beings of Jupiter are utterly different from human beings. Think of a quality which is sometimes more and sometimes less in evidence, namely the quality of *wisdom.* Men insist that they are wise . . . but what a struggle it is for them to acquire wisdom! The tiniest fragment of wisdom in any field is difficult to attain and demands inner effort. Nothing of the kind is necessary for the Jupiter Beings. Wisdom is an integral part of their very nature—I cannot say it is 'born' in them, for the Jupiter Beings do not come into existence through an embryo as men do on Earth. You must picture to yourselves that there is something around Jupiter like the cloud-masses around the Earth. If you were now to imagine bodies of men forming out of the clouds and flying down to the Earth, that would be a picture of how the new Beings come forth from a kind of cloud-mass on Jupiter; but these Beings have wisdom as an original, intrinsic characteristic. Just as we have circulating blood, so they have wisdom. But their wisdom is not a merited reward, nor has it been acquired by effort; they have it by nature. Therefore their thinking, too, is utterly different from the thinking of men. The experience is shattering, overwhelming, but we must gradually get accustomed to the idea. Just as we on Earth are pervaded by air, so everything on Jupiter is pervaded by wisdom. Wisdom there has substantiality, streams in the atmosphere, discharges itself like rain on Jupiter, rises like mist to the heights. But Beings are there—Beings who ascend in a cloud, a mist of wisdom. Herein live the Cherubim, who in this realm of existence gather up and give shape to the karma of human beings. Other impulses too are in operation, but what holds good unconditionally is that the experiences of an earlier incarnation are gathered together and moulded into shape by the forces of the self-subsisting wisdom of the Jupiter sphere. Then, when the individuality comes down again to incarnation on the Earth, he bears the stamp arising from the re-shaping of his earlier experiences by wisdom which ultimately takes effect in very diverse forms.—Again we will take an example.

There is an individuality who leads us back to ancient Greece, into a milieu of Platonism, and also of sculpture. This individuality had a very significant incarnation as a sculptor in Greece. What he there experienced was carried over into intermediate incarnations of less importance. This is an individuality whose karma for what is at the moment his latest incarnation was elaborated chiefly in the sphere of the Jupiter wisdom.

Another individuality takes us back to Central America, to Mexico, in times before European people had migrated to America. He was connected with the then declining Mysteries of the early, original inhabitants of Mexico and came into contact with the Mexican deities at a time when the pupils of the Mysteries still had real and living intercourse with these spiritual Beings. This was karma of a special—not a particularly favourable—kind. These Gods—Quetzalcoatl, Tetzkatlipoka, Taotl—are still mentioned by scholars to-day but hardly more than by name. The individuality of whom I am speaking was closely connected with those Mysteries which, in spite of their decadence, enabled a God such as Taotl or Quetzalcoatl to be a living reality to him. There, in those declining Mysteries, he became thoroughly versed in the magic arts—arts which were already rife with superstition—and a Being like Tetzkatlipoka was a vivid reality to him. Tetzkatlipoka was a kind of Serpent God with whom men felt themselves astrally connected. Unlike the other individuality whose life as a man in Greece was followed by female incarnations, this individuality had no intermediate incarnation. He lived as a man within the Mexican Mysteries, passed through the sphere of the Jupiter-wisdom in his life between death and a new birth and then incarnated in the eighteenth/nineteenth century. The other individuality who had lived in Greece also passed through the Jupiter sphere in the way that is possible for one who had been a sculptor and had unfolded the faculty of creative imagination which was still so potent a force in Greece. This was transformed and re-cast in the Jupiter sphere where the wisdom underlying the Greek talent for plastic representation of the human form, for pictorial conceptions of the world, is present in its very essence, and the individuality came down into a body with a strongly Grecian bent of mind that had been elaborated in the Jupiter sphere, being reborn as *Goethe*.



4—KR * *

The other individuality also passed through the Jupiter sphere, where his experiences in the Mexican Mysteries were cast into a new form. But the Jupiter sphere could not produce identical results from an earthly life in Greece and an earthly life in Mexico of the kinds I have described. Both sets of experience were worked upon by the wisdom of the Jupiter sphere but both were conditioned by the formative forces that had been in operation in earlier lives. The individuality who had been connected with the Mexican Mysteries lived through the Jupiter sphere and was reborn as *Eliphas Levi.* There you have an example of how magic practices, magic rites and enactments have been transformed in a remarkable way into wisdom. It is Jupiter-karma of an inferior kind, but for all that replete with spirituality, replete with wisdom. From this we perceive how what a man has experienced in earthly life works into what he becomes during his life between death and a new birth. The later life is invariably conditioned by the earlier life. But the experiences of earthly life can be transformed by the selfsame sphere into very different karma. Our view of human life can only be deepened in the right way when we perceive how this life is shaped in conformity with karma. Then it is enriched, then and only then do we acquire a real knowledge of man and of human life.

## *Lecture Four*

In the lecture yesterday we began to speak about the connection of man's life on Earth between birth and death with his other life in supersensible worlds between death and a new birth, with special reference to karma. We heard that man works together with other human souls with whom he is karmically connected and with the spiritual Beings of the higher Hierarchies to give shape to his karma and to mould the deeds, thoughts and feelings of an earlier earthly life or a series of lives, in such a way that they become the basis of experiences in a coming incarnation. This knowledge sheds light upon the historical life of humanity itself, inasmuch as every individual—whether his achievments are of outstanding, epoch-making significance or whether he works in limited circles only—is seen against the background of momentous happenings in the spiritual worlds. We were able to realise that human destiny, when we begin to understand it, becomes the outer expression, the earthly expression of stupendous happenings in the spiritual worlds. Thus it is man himself who carries over to a later epoch and brings to fulfilment in that epoch, the effects of experiences lived through in earlier times. The processes connected with historical 'Becoming' are therefore set in operation by man himself, and I think that such a view of history cannot fail to be impressive and uplifting. We shall learn to feel and experience our own karma rightly if to begin with—before entering in the following lectures into matters connected with individual karma—we observe personalities whose lives are more or less common knowledge, and perceive from such examples how the one earthly life works over into subsequent incarnations.

We learned how the spiritual Beings belonging to a planetary sphere and the whole spiritual constitution of that sphere penetrate and work into what a man brings with him when after death he is journeying onward in the spiritual world. Certain things were said about the working of the Jupiter sphere. The Saturn sphere works in a still more drastic way. I told you that even with the insight of Initiation one must have passed the sixty-third year and be able to look back over the period of life between the ages of fifty-six and sixty-three before it is possible to acquire independent vision of all the connections, and, in the setting of the weaving spiritual life of the whole Universe, discern how the Saturn sphere works upon man. The whole working of the Saturn sphere is conditioned by the fact that in all the Beings of this sphere there is an intense, all-pervading consciousness of the *past*, and more or less unconsciousness of the immediate present. This makes a deep and shattering impression. The immediate deeds of the Saturn Beings, even including the deeds of the Seraphim, are performed in a kind of unconsciousness. These Beings are not aware, in the immediate present, of what is happening to them and through them; but they know at once, with unerring exactitude, what they have done, what they have thought, what has taken place among them, directly it has actually happened.

Let me try by means of a picture to characterise the conditions of existence prevailing in the Saturn sphere. Imagine yourselves walking about the Earth, never knowing in the immediately present moment what you are doing, what you are thinking, what is happening to you or through you; you are just walking. As you walk you do not see yourselves, but you leave traces behind; from the spot you reached a moment previously there arises, let us say, a little snow-man; you take another step—another little snow-man is there; a further step—again a little snow-man . . . and so it goes on. Mobile figures are being left behind you all the time and you can look back and see yourselves exactly as you once were. The very moment something has happened through you, you see it there, see how it remains, becomes part of Eternity. You look back and in this perspective see everything that has happened through you inscribed as it were in an eternal chronicle in the Universe. The consciousness of the Saturn Beings is of this character. But what the Saturn Beings behold as a vista of past ages of evolution unites with a vista of the past evolution of all Beings belonging to the entire planetary system. The consciousness of the Saturn Beings may therefore be characterised by saying that they gaze back upon the memory, if I may so express it, of all the Beings of the whole planetary system. Everything is inscribed in this faculty of cosmic remembrance, cosmic memory, of the Saturn Beings. If the vista of the weaving life and realities of existence in the Saturn sphere is a shattering experience for the initiated observer, it is even more shattering for him to perceive how the effects of a previous incarnation are carried down into a new earthly life by individualities whose karma, determined by their particular experiences, was shaped and given configuration in the Saturn sphere. And when this is revealed in a personality of outstanding importance in world-history, our vista of the Universe takes on a content of untold majesty and power.

If we study the life of such personalities here on Earth—that is to say, if we study it spiritually, not merely figuring out letters of a script but reading its meaning—we are led to the realities of existence in the Saturn sphere. Our conceptual life is infinitely enriched in spiritual content when the workings of the Saturn sphere are revealed; we look down to the Earth and perceive in happenings there a reflected image of what occurred in the Saturn sphere.

There is an individuality who lived in the South of Europe in the first century A.D., at the time when Hellenism was still a potent influence in the development of Christianity, and who with strong intellectual leanings to Hellenised Christianity passed through experiences in the Roman Empire that were of common occurrence during those early centuries. He witnessed the cruel persecutions of the Christians, the brutalities of Roman Imperialism, the unjust treatment meted out to the better types of men. Filled with profound indignation by these happenings, he passed through the gate of death in a mood of despair and resignation, questioning whether there is any hope of progress for a world in which such things are possible. Having witnessed the evil deeds of the Caesars and the sacrifices of individual Christian martyrs, doubt arose in this soul as to whether there is any prospect at all of ultimate adjustment between good and evil in the world. The spectacle of the good on the one side and of the evil on the other stood before him in dire and often terrible contrast. With this impression the soul passed through the gate of death and subsequently through less important earthly lives. But the experiences of the Graeco-Roman incarnation had engraved deep furrows in the life of soul and it was these experiences which, as the eighteenth century approached, were elaborated and wrought out in the Saturn sphere into the subsequent karma of this individuality. The Saturn sphere has a deep and incisive effect upon the shaping of karma. Whenever it is a case of laying hold of the human soul in its very depths and of developing radical, potent forces from these depths, the Saturn sphere works in such a way that the forces will penetrate deeply, very deeply into the physical organisation. Everything that happens in the Saturn sphere is intrinsically and essentially spiritual but also takes far deeper effect when the human being descends to earthly embodiment. The result is a physical organisation which strives for a balancing-out of the experiences undergone by the soul in an earlier earthly life. The element of retrospection is always strongly at work. When a man's karma is being wrought out in the Saturn sphere he looks backwards, to remembrances, to the past. Then, when he comes down to the earthly realm, the negative image as it were of what he has lived through in the Saturn sphere discloses itself. The intense concentration upon the past is transformed into a resolute striving for ideals which lead forward, towards the *future*. Human beings who bring down their karma from the Saturn sphere are fired with enthusiasm for the future, for ideals which point to the future, precisely because in a purely spiritual life in the Saturn sphere their gaze was directed paramountly to the *past*. The individuality of whom I am here speaking appeared again in the second half of the eighteenth century *Friedrich Schiller.*

Think of Schiller's whole life, think how it comes to expression in the tremendous forcefulness and fire of the early dramas, with their possibly faulty artistic construction, and side by side with this, think of the deep seriousness, the profound melancholy that weighed upon his soul. See how everything in Schiller, especially the pathos of his early destiny, emanates from the vein of melancholy that is so deeply rooted in his soul. And then, when he becomes acquainted with Goethe, see how he unfolds a kind of inspired understanding of Hellenism; see all this as the foreground and behind it the man whose outlook acquired its basic trend on the one side in the early centuries of Hellenised Christianity and on the other from the horror and indignation aroused by the behaviour of the Roman Emperors, and then see how these experiences are deepened and wrought out into new karma by the forces of the Saturn sphere. Schiller is through and through a Saturn man in respect of his karma.—These things are not rightly experienced if they are regarded as so many theories. They can be truly grasped only by one who with all the forces of his heart and mind steeps himself in the realities of this spiritual life and being in the starry worlds—in this case, the Saturn sphere—and having acquired a deeper understanding of an individual earthly destiny, observes them in manifestation there.

I will give you another example where the working of destiny again took quite a different form. One can perceive an individuality who in a preceding earthly life had reached a certain degree of Initiation. But before I speak of this particular karma, I must enunciate a question which will have occurred to everyone who thinks about such matters and which many of you will certainly have put to yourselves. It is the question that arises when in our anthroposophical studies we hear that in the course of the earthly evolution of humanity there have been Initiates, men initiated into the great secrets of existence and of earthly wisdom, to whom we look up with deepest respect and veneration. When we speak of repeated earthly lives, the question may be raised about the reincarnation of these Initiates. It may be asked: Have they, then, not reincarnated in the present age? Is it a fact that at the present time the Initiates have withdrawn entirely from the world in which we ourselves are living between birth and death? This is by no means the case; but it must not be forgotten that when a human being comes down from pre-earthly existence in realms of soul-and-spirit into an earthly life, he is dependent upon the physical body, the education and so forth, which a particular epoch can provide. The individuality who reincarnates on the Earth must submit to all these conditions. We may certainly be able to observe some Initiate belonging, let us say, to a very distant past, whose karma it is to be born again in the eighteenth or nineteenth century. But in the eighteenth century there were no bodies on Earth in the least like the bodies of remote antiquity which were so pliable and therefore readily adaptable to the spiritual individuality. The view that the human body has not changed since time immemorial is due to a deterioration of knowledge. In the age of materialism the body has become hard, unyielding, stiff, not easily manipulated. The hereditary relationships which are also connected with the disposition, the whole inner soul-constitution of man, are as they are, and the individual can do nothing to alter them; the whole of civilisation stands in the way and the individual must submit. The nature of these hereditary relationships is such that part of what a man has carried over in his soul from an ancient Initiation cannot be brought down into the physical organism and for this reason cannot be raised to the level of consciousness; for man can bring into the outer consciousness prevailing in a given epoch only that which he has been able to carry right down into the physical body. And here I shall have to say something highly paradoxical, but you must accept it because it is the truth.

In ages of remote antiquity the Initiates were preserved from something that is nowadays a great boon for the human race. If they had been subjected to it in those times it would have been regarded as anything but a boon, on the contrary as a great hindrance to Initiation. It is not permissible now to prevent anyone from learning in the modern way to read and write. But as a matter of fact one loses a great deal through being forced to adopt these alphabetical ciphers to which one has no human relationship whatever. When the more civilised Europeans showed the letters of their alphabet to the uncultured American Indians, the latter were frightened by what they took to be so many little kobolds, little demons. This will show you what it means to introduce to a human being something that is so unnatural, so alien to him at the age of six or seven, as the letters of our script—for I ask you, has an A or a B in the form that is thrust upon us as children any relation to human life? It has none, not the very remotest! In ancient Egypt there were at least hieroglyphs, and the picture that was painted or drawn did bear some suggestion of resemblance to the reality; moreover men were made conscious of the relation between the picture and the reality. But to-day we learn A, B, C, as something entirely remote from life. Those who want to judge everything materialistically, to live in the world only with the ordinary, everyday consciousness, cannot possibly realise all that is driven out of the human being, what is really killed in him as the result of having to learn this A, B, C, this reading and writing, by modern methods. (In the Waldorf School we are trying to rectify the worst mistakes in education and so, among other things, we have introduced a different way of teaching reading and writing.)

The fact that when I was fifteen years old I was still unable to spell accurately has certainly been a shock to others, but never to me personally. I have spoken at some length on the subject in *The Story of my Life*, and I owe much to this fact. For it meant that I was protected from many things against which there is no protection if by the age of fifteen one's spelling is orthographically perfect. Many things that are the outcome of the materialistic education of our day sever the human being from the spiritual life. This is a far more serious matter than people think. I mention it here in order to show you that an Initiate of bygone times has no other alternative than to avail himself of the kind of education that a particular epoch has to offer. What else can he do but adapt himself to the life of body and soul belonging to the times? True, he is obliged to let many things in his life of soul lie in the background. But for all that, from signs which may come into evidence at a certain age in his life, it will certainly be possible, even in the case of one who outwardly appears again as an ordinary citizen of the Earth and not at all as an Initiate, to discern the karmic connection with earlier Initiation. What works in karma is *not* what is thought, on the face of it, to be the outstanding feature in a man's life. For instance, in the case of someone with a very definite stamp of mind, one is readily inclined, if karma is being judged merely from the intellectual standpoint, to trace it back to similar quality in the previous earthly life. But this does not hold good. The karmic forces that become free and work over from one earthly life into the other, lie in a region of the soul far, far deeper than that of the intellectual makeup. I need only give an example and you will see that what influences karma proceeds from quite other regions of the life of soul than those from which the intellect derives.

*Ernst Haeckel* was undoubtedly a most interesting personality of the nineteenth century. What struck people most forcibly about him was his materialistic view of the world, his fight against Ultramontanism, against the Papacy and the Roman Catholic Church. Haeckel worked himself into such a pitch of fervour in this fight that the expressions he used, although at times very refreshing, were at others lacking in taste. When his karma is traced back into the past, one finds him, in his most important previous incarnation, as Pope Gregory the Great, the mighty Pope who strove to establish the external, worldly supremacy of the Papacy as against that of the Emperors. Pope Gregory the Great, as Hildebrand, had come from the Cluniac Order which from the sixth until the thirteenth century had been engaged in a struggle with Rome, until one of its own members actually became Pope. To begin with, he too, in his own way, was actively at variance with the Papacy in the form it had assumed in those days. What worked over from the Hildebrand incarnation into the Haeckel incarnation was the enthusiasm for pressing home a certain world-conception, enthusiasm for the realisation of impulses arising from a particular view of the world. This is only an example to disprove the belief that it is possible to discover an earlier incarnation of importance by external observation of a particular constitution of soul. Caution is necessary in these matters, and attention must be given to what often seem to be trifling idiosyncracies. If these are discerned with spiritual insight they will gradually provide the clue to the content of the earlier earthly life.

Saturn-karma—Saturn-karma above all—works in deep, very deep regions of the soul. I want now to direct your attention to an individuality who in an earlier incarnation was actually an Initiate. I speak very objectively in this case and it has cost me a good deal of effort to work through to the truth because I was never specially attracted by this individuality in his new incarnation, nor am I to-day. But it is a matter of establishing objective facts and although effort is necessary, the truth is that one can discern with greater prospects of exactitude the karma of individuals to whom one is not drawn by personal sympathy and the like. And so I am going to speak to you about an individuality who in an earlier earthly life was an Initiate in Mysteries which were of very great moment in the evolution of humanity. This individuality was an Initiate in Irish Mysteries, the Mysteries of Hibernia, to which I have referred in one of the Mystery Plays. There were many experiences to be undergone before a man was led onwards through Initiation to wisdom in the form in which it was presented to him in these Irish Mysteries. The aspirant for Initiation had first to experience every kind of doubt that can arise in the human soul concerning the great truths of existence. The pupil was actually taught to doubt, to be utterly sceptical of everything, especially of the highest truths. And only when he had undergone all the suffering, the sense of tragedy, dejection and inner despair which accompany such doubt, only then was he guided to a full comprehension of truth, first of all as an Imaginative, pictorial experience and then as an experience of spiritual reality. Thus everyone who attained Initiation in the Hibernian Mysteries had learned not only to believe in the truth but also *not* to believe in it. Only so could his fidelity to truth prove itself a potent, unshakable force in life. Another feeling too was awakened in those who sought the Initiation-wisdom of Hibernia. It was the feeling that all existence may be as earthly existence: illusory, unreal. The pupils were brought to a point where they not only doubted truth but where they experienced the nothingness, the non-reality in human existence. And then, in order that the pupil might experience the etheric forces in their constant transformations and the physical forces which though involved in destruction are ever and again restored by the Spiritual, in order that when the right state of soul had been induced he might experience in a real imagination the destructive and upbuilding forces implicit in all life, he was led before two mighty pillar-statues. He was exhorted to press into one of the statues; this caused an indentation but because the substance of this statue was elastic throughout the form was ever and again restored and the statue seemed as though it were alive. And because the impression made by the actual touch was received by the pupil in a mood of reverence and solemnity, he became aware, inwardly aware, of the essential nature of the Living. The other statue was so constructed that pressure left an indentation which defaced the form and it was not until the following day, when the pupil was again led before this statue, that the deformation was repaired. The inner constitution of the Physical and the Etheric—something therefore of the truth revealed to self-observation—was presented in this way to the pupils. Then they were taken before other images and were thus led on to an even fuller understanding. The experience of spiritual reality was strong and intense in the pupils and Initiates of Hibernia. Indeed at certain stages of Initiation they no longer paid much heed to outer, physical reality, so intensely conscious were they of spiritual reality. It is actually the case that while the Mystery of Golgotha was taking place in physical reality over in Asia, the Hibernian priesthood so conducted the ceremonies that at the very time when the Mystery of Golgotha was fulfilled in outer, physical reality in Palestine, it was enacted in the form of a sacred rite in a Mystery Centre of Hibernia. Thus a physical fact taking place in a different region of the Earth was experienced in distant Hibernia as a *spiritual* fact. This will show you to what depths men were led in those Hibernian Mysteries.

There is an individuality who in very early times had attained a certain degree of Initiation in the Hibernian Mysteries and then, later on, passed through a female incarnation—but the influence of the Hibernian incarnation worked deeply, very deeply upon the soul. Then, in a life between death and a new birth, this individuality lived through experiences arising when karma is wrought out in the Saturn sphere. The whole significance of what the soul had acquired in an Hibernian Initiation—not at the highest but at a certain stage—was seen in retrospect, in a perspective widening out into a vista of great cosmic happenings. The import of the knowledge which it was possible to acquire in Hibernia was seen in its relation to the whole past evolution of man. In a majestic vision of cosmic evolution it was revealed how human longings and strivings through thousands of years had brought this Hibernia into being. But the modern age held in store for this individuality a body and a kind of education by which the most significant elements were obscured—yet for all that came to a certain expression in keeping with the civilisation of the nineteenth century. In this case too, what had been retained of the great cosmic retrospect was transformed when the soul came down into a physical body and underwent a kind of education neither of which in truth were suited to experiences lived through in an Hibernian Initiation and wrought out in the Saturn sphere. When the soul descended, this was all transformed into ideals reaching out to the future. But because the body was that of a Frenchman of the nineteenth century and therefore altogether different from the remarkable bodies of the old Irish Initiates, a very great deal receded into the background, transforming itself into sublime but fantastic pictures which, however have a certain power, a certain grandeur about them. This individuality reincarnated as *Victor Hugo*.

There again we can perceive how karma works on, even when two incarnations differ as greatly as do the lives of the Irish Initiate and Victor Hugo. For it is *not* in external similarities that we must seek for evidence of the working of karma; rather must we be observant of those things which in the deep foundations of a man's being are carried over through karma from one earthly life into another. Perception of the karma of an individual human being, or even of one's own karma, requires the right attitude, the right mood-of soul. The whole study of karma is profaned if this study is pursued in the attitude of mind arising from our modern education and civilisation. The mood in which all teachings about karma should be received is one of piety, of reverence. Whenever man approaches a truth relating to karma, his soul should feel as though part of the veil of Isis were being lifted. For in truth it is karma that reveals, in a way most intimately connected with human life, what Isis was—the Being designated outwardly as: 'I am that which was, is, and will be.' This must still be the attitude of soul in all study of human karma. In truth, only when we study karma in the way we have now been doing and having observed how it takes effect in the process of world-evolution acquire the reverence befitting such study, then and only then can we gaze with the right attitude of soul at what may be our own karma, perceiving how from earlier earthly lives it has unfolded and taken shape as a result of experiences in the spiritual worlds of the stars between death and a new birth. With our whole being we gaze at supersensible worlds when we 'read' karma with the right mood-of-soul. For the study of karma acquaints us with laws that are in utter contrast with the laws of external Nature. In the external world, Nature-relationships hold sway, but these must be discarded entirely and we must be able to gaze at spirit-relationships if we are to discern the law operating in the working of karma. Clearly, the best preparation for this will be to study illuminating examples of karma in world-history, in order that light may be shed upon things that are of importance to us in living out and observing our own karma. By speaking of characteristic personalities to illustrate the working of karma in world-history, I wanted to prepare you for other such studies during the next few days.

## *Lecture Five*

As our studies continue we shall gradually come to understand what karma may signify in the individual life of man, although I shall constantly be drawing attention to certain karmic connections of personalities known in history. For if we observe the manifestations of karma across the wide perspective of history, light will also be shed upon details of our own karma which cannot fail to interest us. At the very outset let it be said that clairvoyant insight is not essential to the perception, the feeling, of the working of karma. It is quite true that in order to survey the whole range of karmic laws such insight is necessary; and much that I have been telling you during the last few days can, of course, be discovered only by means of clairvoyance. But the feeling, the clear and distinct feeling for karma is a preparation for clairvoyant insight. This feeling and perception can play a part in the life of every individual provided that he is not exclusively concerned with superficialities and outwardly sensational happenings, but unfolds a sensitive understanding of the more intimate experiences of existence and an inkling of certain connections of destiny which by their very nature show that they cannot possibly be rooted in the one earthly life between birth and death.

Let us think of how we meet and become acquainted with other human beings. By far the greatest part of our destiny depends upon these meetings. We meet one person or another and the experiences we share with him have an effect upon our life. And precisely the experiences we share with others in different circumstances of life will make it evident to attentive observation that karma is not irreconcilable with the ingrained feeling of the extent to which our actions are the outcome of free decision. After all, we are sent into existence in an epoch of life when as far as earthly impulses are concerned there can be no question of freedom. A very great deal depends upon how we are placed in existence as children. The faculties that are drawn out of us, the paths along which we are directed—all this is of infinite significance in the destiny of our whole life. Later on, as independent human beings, we can of course take a hand in directing our own existence but even then the place assigned to us in childhood is determinative. And so if we observe closely we shall certainly be able to perceive how destiny plays into our free actions, our free deeds and activities.

Think of the following.—We meet other human beings and there is clearly a difference between one kind of acquaintanceship and another. We may meet someone for the first time and feel at once that there is a bridge leading over from our soul to his. We may well be strongly drawn to him but not nearly as interested in the details of his outward appearance, whether he is handsome or ugly, whether he looks friendly or ill-disposed. What draws us to him is something that wells up from within us; we feel sympathy towards him. In the case of another person we may actually feel antipathy simply when we are near him and conscious of his presence. Our feeling for him does not depend upon the impression he makes through his actions or what he actually says to us. Such experiences stand in earthly existence like question-marks, like far-reaching problems set us by reality. With both these kinds of acquaintanceship we feel no urge at all to ask: what is the individual *really* like? What does he actually do? Everything that attracts us to him gathers into an aggregate of feelings arising from experiences and components of our soul-life, feelings which there is no need to justify by what he actually does.

But there are acquaintanceships of a different kind, where no such experiences occur. Although there is no feeling of deep-seated sympathy or antipathy, such individuals interest us. We feel an urge to discover whether their attitude is friendly or unfriendly, whether they are gifted or not gifted. Having made such an acquaintanceship it may happen that we meet someone who also knows the person in question and we feel we want to talk about him, to ask about his position in life, who he is, and so forth; we are interested in what he is outwardly. But in connection with an acquaintance of the other category we may find it extremely embarrassing to meet someone who knows him and begins to speak about him. We simply do not want to talk about this person. Now when Spiritual Science endeavours to get to the root of an occurrence of this nature, it turns out that if an inexplicable feeling of affection or dislike wells up in us when we meet a particular person, then we have had some karmic tie with him in the past and this has really guided our whole path in such a way that at a certain moment in life we come across him. Experiences shared in past ages shape and determine the feelings we have about him. And it is these feelings that count—not whether he is good-looking or ugly, kindly or ill-disposed. When such feelings are emphatic and distinct and it is possible for spiritual-scientific investigation to shed light upon them, their explanation is forthcoming from what such investigation has to say about karma that was formed in the *past*. Moreover we shall find this confirmed in many other ways.

During sleep, when we are outside our physical and etheric bodies, living a spiritual existence in the 'I' and astral body, dreams occur. But with rigorous self-observation let us ask ourselves whether it is not the case, when certain acquaintanceships are accompanied by these uprising feelings and experiences, that we at once begin to dream about these people. We dream so readily about certain acquaintances. This indicates that there is a connection between the person in question and our own soul-and-spirit which has shared experiences with him either in many lives or maybe in one life only; our 'I' and astral body in which we live during sleep, are connected in some way with this individual. Others whom we may encounter in our profession, business or the like, interest us in the different way I described. It may well happen that we have a great deal to do with them; life throws us together, but we simply cannot dream about them. In such cases the connection belongs only to the *present* earthly life and the link is made by what binds the soul-and-spiritual part of man to the physical and the etheric. Now it is paramountly the physical and etheric bodies which are involved in interests connected with external activities, outward appearances, and the reason why we cannot dream about these particular people is that the physical and etheric bodies lie there in the bed and the being of soul-and-spirit is not within them. Spiritual Science reveals that although karma is certainly at work here it is only now beginning to form and that not until we look back from spiritual existence upon this earthly life will it be possible to say that karmic connections *began* in that life. In this case, karma is in process of coming into being.

We have heard how karma takes shape, how all that we experience in communion with spiritual Beings between death and a new birth works for long ages at the weaving of karma. But if you reflect upon what has here been said about the laws of karma, you will say to yourselves: earthly life brings human beings together and a karmic link is formed between them; they pass together through the life between death and rebirth and in cooperation with higher Beings shape their karma for the next earthly life. What, then, is the consequence in the earthly life of man? Broadly speaking this: that individuals who have been together in an earthly life where karma begins to form, will endeavour in the next earthly life to find their way to one another again. Once again they will establish karmic links, will again pass through the life between death and rebirth where a still stronger link is forged between them, and again seek for a common earthly existence. And here the remarkable fact comes to light that as Earth-evolution runs its course, human beings live together in groups. Time flows on: a certain group of human beings living as contemporaries in a particular epoch and karmically connected with one another, appears again on the Earth after the life spent between death and rebirth. A different group of human beings linked together by karmic ties appears on the Earth in a common existence; a third group likewise. As the periods between death and rebirth are by far the longer, it follows that the majority of human beings only meet in the life after death and before birth and that those specially connected with one another by karma pass through evolution in groups, coming together again and again on the Earth. That is the general rule. *As a rule* it is the case that on Earth we do not encounter those who formerly were *not* incarnated at the same time as ourselves.

We learn that this is so when with spiritual insight we ponder upon the facts and consequences of human relationships. Provided we reflect without prejudices or preconceptions, spiritual observation will certainly confirm what has here been said.—As you know, for a considerable time in my early life I was engrossed in the study of Goethe. I had this spiritual preoccupation with Goethe so much at heart that I often asked myself: What if I had been a contemporary of Goethe? Outwardly, the prospect would have been entrancing! For when one is strongly drawn to Goethe, loves to steep oneself in his works and devotes part of one's life to elucidating and interpreting him, how could one fail to think of how delightful it would have been to have lived in Weimar at the same time, to have seen him, perhaps even to have been able to converse with him. But that, after all, is a superficial point of view which deeper insight immediately corrects. At all events I realised that the very thought of living as a contemporary of Goethe would be quite unbearable. For one treasured Goethe so highly just because the creations he bequeathed had worked in one for a time and it was then possible to draw it all forth again from spiritual depths of world-existence. To have lived as a contemporary of Goethe would have been unbearable! When it is clear that the relationship was the result of having been born at a later time, when the subtler connections of the life of soul are taken into account in a case like this where one is drawn to a personality with whom karma did not bring one into direct contact, where the karmic relationships are more complicated, it becomes clear to spiritual insight that had one lived at the same time as this personality, he would have acted like poison upon the soul. I know that this is a strong statement, but it is a fact, nevertheless. To have been a contemporary of Goethe would have made it impossible to keep one's own disposition and configuration of soul firmly knit.

From the wider point of view such circumstances sharpen our perception of the inner truths, the inner relationships, of human life. We no longer talk out of the blue nor shall we be tempted to come out with the hackneyed exclamation: 'Oh, if only I had been alive then!' When karma is interpreted rightly, it becomes a source of strength in the circumstances of our life, establishes us in earthly existence at the place where we truly belong. That karma is in truth *destiny* becomes plain when we begin to reflect upon why we were born at a particular time. We come into earthly existence just when we do, because together with other souls who are karmically connected with us we have prepared our karma for the time when we are to descend to physical existence on Earth.

What I have been telling you is the general rule—but in the spiritual world everything is *individual.* Rules have their significance but this must not be taken to imply that they are to be regarded as principles. A man who is a stickler for rules, who insists that they can have no exceptions, will never find his way into the spiritual world. For in the spiritual world nothing is the same as it is in the physical world. What could be more obvious to a man living in the physical world than the mathematical axiom: the whole is greater than any of its parts—or the straight way is the shortest distance between two points? Only a lunatic would contend that the whole is not greater than any of its parts. Such things are called 'axioms' because they are self-evident truths and, as it is said, cannot and need not be proved. The same applies to the formula: the straight way is the shortest distance between any two points. But neither formula holds good in the spiritual world. What actually holds good in the spiritual world is the formula: the whole is always *smaller* than any one of its parts. And we find confirmation of this in the very being of man. Observed in the spiritual world, the spiritual counterpart of your physical being is about the size—a trifle larger but approximately the same size as it is in the physical world. When, however, you see your lungs or your liver in the spiritual world, they are of gigantic magnitude, and yet they are parts of something small. We have to learn to change our thinking entirely. In the spiritual world the straight way is by no means the shortest but on the contrary the very longest, because in that world to move from one point to another is a different matter altogether. In the physical world it is pedantically correct to say: that way is long, this longer, this—the straight—the shortest. But in the spiritual world the straight way presents such enormous difficulties that any of the winding ways is the shorter. Hence there is no sense in saying: the straight way is the shortest between any two points—because in actual fact it is the longest of all.

We have to recognise that in the spiritual world nothing is the same as in the physical world. The reason why people find it so difficult to reach the spiritual world with the exercises they practise quite faithfully is that they cling to preconceptions such as: the whole is greater than any of its parts, or, the straight way is the shortest between two points. So much for the axioms.

But we must also give up clinging to all other truths which hold good in the physical world if we are to penetrate into the spiritual world. In the spiritual world there can be no all-embracing principles, for everything there is individual. Each fact must be approached as something entirely individual. In the spiritual world there is none of this dreadful, logical assembling of facts, this basing of everything upon general rules. And so the truth of which I have spoken, namely, that human beings pass through their earthly evolution in groups—although it is indeed a truth and holds good in the broad sense—is sometimes broken through. And precisely from those cases where it is broken through we can realise its significance. Let me give an example.

You must forgive these examples being taken from my own life. After all, how can there be closer knowledge of examples of these things than when they are drawn from one's own life? In recounting the story of my life I have mentioned a geometry teacher of mine. Not only had I great affection for this teacher while I was actually his pupil, but afterwards too, and it was interesting for me to investigate his karma and the whole setting of his life. I myself had a personal weakness, as the saying goes, for geometry. Even at the age of nine, a geometry book that fell into my hands brought me sheer delight; it was written by this teacher who thought me far too immature for anything of the kind. To learn that the three angles of a triangle total 180° was sheer joy to me when I was a boy of nine. But later on, when I was about twelve, and for some years after, this man was my geometry teacher. He was a most remarkable and interesting personality, for he was, so to say, the very embodiment of geometry—but of a particular kind: descriptive, constructive geometry. In the higher classes I was obliged to learn analytical geometry—as it is called—from others, because my former teacher simply did not understand it. He was a first-rate constructor and in that branch he was wonderfully impressive. I myself made remarkable progress in geometry just because I loved him so deeply. It was always a happy hour for me when this teacher came into the class and demonstrated geometry in his own characteristic way. Later on—because my interest in him never waned—I realised that it was only natural to investigate the karmic setting of his life. Now when it is a matter of investigating karma, one can get nowhere by focusing attention upon what, at first sight, makes the most striking impression. If I had paid attention only to his excellence as a teacher of geometry, I should certainly never have discovered the threads of his karma. But what made a deep impression upon me in connection with his life was the fact that he had a club-foot. One leg was shorter than the other. These are details which in the ordinary way are thought to have no bearing upon the actual life. The things of really deep interest, however, are those which lead to the karmic connections. They need not necessarily be very striking. One may actually be led to a man's karmic connection by some repeated habit. A trifling habit may form itself into a picture and lead one to the karmic connections in earlier lives of the person concerned. And so in the case of another teacher for whom I had great affection, I was guided to certain karmic connections—of which I do not now propose to speak—through the fact that whenever this teacher came to his class, the first thing he did was to take out his handkerchief and blow his nose! He never by any chance began a lesson without doing this, and the picture into which this habit shaped itself led me back to his earlier earthly lives. And it was the same with the other teacher, the one with the club-foot. In point of fact it was this club-foot which gave me the first clue to his particular talent. It is usually thought that the ability to construct figures from geometrical lines comes from the head. But that is simply not the case. Man does not experience geometry through his head. You would never be able to think of an angle if you did not *walk*. It is because you experience the angle in your legs that you know something about it. The head merely looks on, perceives how the arms or the legs form angles. In geometry we actually experience our own will weaving through our limbs. *Our limbs* teach us geometry. It is only because we have become such creatures of abstraction that we are unaware of this and firmly believe that all geometrising goes on in the head. The head looks on. perceives how we walk, or dance, or whatever it may be. and then evolves the geometrical figures. And now the whole connection, the reason for this characteristic way of presenting geometry, was clear to me as I studied the inner constitution of this man who was obliged to walk about with a club-foot and who because of the deep effect it had upon him became such an excellent geometrician—but in one direction only. Such things belong to the more intimate concatenations of life.

But what led me to further insight? Coupled with this teacher there arose before me the picture of another man, also with a club-foot, namely, the English poet, *Lord Byron*. The two men with this physical similarity came in a picture before me, side by side, and many things that had played over from earlier karma into the moral and ethical connections of Byron's life but had also come to expression in his club-foot, became clear to me. When perception of karma has reached this point, its range widens and I was now able to discover that these two men had lived as companions in Eastern Europe at a certain time during the Middle Ages; they had shared a similar destiny and the content of their lives at that time was revealed to me.

Neither the earlier life of Byron nor that of my teacher resembled their lives in the nineteenth century. But the two had been associated in destiny of a very intimate kind. During their lives in Eastern Europe they came to know of the significant legend concerning the palladium—the treasure endowed with magical power upon which the might of Troy depended. The palladium had been buried in Troy and was an object of veneration there. Then it was taken across Africa to Rome where it remained for long ages. When he founded Constantinople, the Emperor Constantine caused this palladium—upon which the power, first of Troy and then of Rome was said to depend—to be removed at the cost of great hardships and with tremendous pomp, to Constantinople, where it was sunk in the ground, in order that the power of Constantinople should replace that of Rome. It is said—and with considerable truth—that the Emperor's arrogance had caused him to transfer the palladium from Rome to Constantinople where he erected a massive column over the spot at which it had been sunk and had a statue of Apollo placed upon this column. The task of bringing the column to Constantinople was one of enormous difficulty, entailing the construction of a special road. The column had originally been brought from Egypt to Rome and its weight was so enormous that every road to Constantinople subsided and became dangerous. The column was erected and the palladium safely protected. The Emperor ordered the statue of Apollo to be set in place but let it be known that this statue was a representation of himself. Then, having caused wood and nails from the Cross of Christ to be brought from the East, he had the wood inserted into the statue and the nails moulded into rays around the head of Apollo. Constantine pictured himself standing there aloft, surrounded by rays of glory fashioned from the wood and the nails of the Cross of Christ. Later on, another legend came to be associated with the palladium, a legend which still played a part in the Testament of Peter the Great, to the effect that the palladium would be carried off by men of the East to their capital, that in time to come the power of the Slavs would be founded on its magical power; through the palladium, so it was said, power would pass to the Slavs just as it had passed to Troy, to Rome, to Constantinople. Such things contain deep truths, even though they are presented in the form of legend.

But this much is certain: anyone who understands the history of the palladium will understand very much of the course taken by European history. This legend came to the knowledge of the two men of whom I have spoken—Byron and his contemporary in the early Middle Ages—and they resolved to seize the palladium and take it to the North, to Russia. They did not succeed; the project failed, as indeed it was bound to do. But something of it remained in the two men; in karmic connections, something remained in them in a strange and remarkable way. At a later time, Byron sought for the palladium in a different fashion; he allied himself with the movement for liberty in Greece—it was the search for a spiritual palladium. This was the urge that had remained in him from the time of which I spoke. And it was clear to anyone who observed my teacher closely, that in spite of his relatively unimportant position, in whatever situation he might be, he evinced an inflexible sense for freedom which was deeply connected in his inmost being with the bodily defect—just as in the case of the one who was his earlier contemporary.

What, then, had happened to these two men? Their paths had separated and they did not find one another again. One of them was Lord Byron, the famous poet; the other, who lived at a slightly later time, was the unknown geometry teacher. In that case the rule of which I have spoken was broken through. But in a curious way, life itself brought me confirmation of this. The teacher I loved so deeply, eagerly awaiting him whenever he came to give his geometry lesson, never once gave me an opportunity of a private conversation with him during the whole of the time he was my teacher. He was like a personality of whom I had only read in history. He did not really fit into the times; one got the impression that he was misplaced in his epoch. Later on, when for the purpose of an anthroposophical lecture I visited the town where he was living in retirement, I looked for his name in the directory. I felt that he must be there and now, after such a lapse of time—thirty years or so—I had a desire to talk to him personally, as a friend. By this time he was quite elderly and lived in Graz, the Austrian home of many University pensioners. I went to Graz for the lecture, found his name in the directory and made up my mind to call on him. But visits from others prevented me, even then, from any private talk with him. Although I loved him so dearly, he remained a shadow-personality in my life. When I went to Graz a second time, I again wanted to visit him, but he had since died. And so here I was confronted with a personality who although I felt so near to him, seemed to be like someone I had merely read about, someone who belonged to a quite different epoch. The circumstances were something like this: I was a contemporary of his but had no karmic connection with him. In none of his earlier incarnations had he been a contemporary of mine. This last life was plainly outside the sequence of the karmic groups to which he really belonged. This was also confirmed by the other case. There had been a departure from the sequence of incarnations to which my teacher belonged because in this earthly life he was not connected with the individual with whom he had formerly been associated. Byron and he did not meet. I am telling you these things in order to show you how karma works and how, by deeper observation, precisely through experiences which, to begin with, are bound to be riddles—and life, after all, is full of riddles—one can really perceive the mysterious weaving of karma. But just as certain contemporaries seem to be only pictures because they have moved out of their own karmic sequence, on the other hand one is fully aware that by far the greater majority of human beings are placed in their epoch by strong, inner necessity. This is often very clear in the case of historical personalities.

Here again, let me give an example. Garibaldi, the champion of liberty in Italy, is a well-known figure. His was in truth a remarkable life. As a personality, Garibaldi attracted me as little as the one I mentioned yesterday, whose karma I investigated. It was in the course of research, and not until then, that I began to be more drawn to Garibaldi. Before I had investigated his karmic connections a great deal about him had seemed to me to be unnatural, hollow—which he most certainly was not. This personality, in spite of being intensely active in politics and practical affairs, seems, when one observes him closely, to stand in a strange way outside life—as if he were living in a purely imagined world, as if he were hovering a little above the Earth. Practical as he was, Garibaldi was also an idealist, as is clear even from his external life. We need only think of a few characteristic episodes in Garibaldi's life and this is at once obvious.—I will speak briefly because time is getting on.—It was by no means an everyday occurrence for a young man to sail around the Adriatic Sea in the first half of the nineteenth century—Garibaldi was born in 1807—at a time when its waters were so fraught with danger. He fell more than once into the hands of pirates and freed himself again after perilous adventures. Occasionally, of course, something of the kind may also happen to others, but it certainly does not occur often, as it did to Garibaldi, that when a man has been for a time beyond the reach of newspapers and finally gets hold of one, he reads in it the announcement of his own death sentence! That was what happened to Garibaldi. He had returned from some maritime adventure and without knowing it had been accused of participating in certain political conspiracies. Sentence of death had been passed upon him in his absence and he read this in the newspaper. He seemed through his destiny to stand a little above actual life.

But other events in his life are even more unusual. Thus, for example, it happened that as the ship in which he had sailed to a foreign country in order to share in certain struggles for freedom, was nearing the coast, he looked through a telescope at the land. There he saw a young, attractive girl and forthwith fell in love with her—through the telescope! It is certainly not the normal way of falling in love. People who are firmly grounded in life do not fall in love through a telescope! But Garibaldi fell head over heels in love and brought his ship with all speed to the spot where he had caught sight of the girl. When he arrived she had vanished, but a man standing there took such a liking to him that he invited him to a meal—it turned out that he was the father of the very girl with whom Garibaldi had fallen in love through the telescope! Thus Garibaldi was able to partake of the meal in the girl's company. He could speak only Italian, she only Portuguese, but both of them understood the language of the heart and they became betrothed. Their life together demanded great valiance on the part of the woman. She accompanied him on his campaigns, acting throughout with great heroism. The circumstances are by no means usual! The first child is born while the husband is many leagues distant and while the wife searches for him on the battlefield she has to strap the child round her neck with a rope in order to keep it warm. She hears that her husband has been killed, faces every imaginable danger in search of him, but finally finds him alive. In spite of everything it was a marriage altogether to be admired. Those familiar with Garibaldi's biography will be aware that the wife predeceased him by a long time and a year after her death, as not infrequently happens, he again became betrothed and married another woman, just like any conventional citizen. This marriage, which was an accomplished fact, lasted only one day and the two separated. Quite obviously, Garibaldi's connection with earthly existence was different from that of other men, and it interested me to investigate a life such as this.

The research led me once again to the Irish Mysteries.

Garibaldi too was an individuality who had passed through the Mysteries of Hibernia. Having reached a certain degree of Initiation, he journeyed eastwards, actually working together with others, in the Rhineland. But in respect of karma, what interested me particularly in the life of Garibaldi was that here was a personality whose activities are really difficult to explain. For in a certain sense Garibaldi was the very personification of sincerity. In the deepest fibres of his being, in his whole attitude of soul, he was a Republican—yet in spite of this it was actually through him that Victor Emanuel came to sit on the Throne of Italy. Garibaldi championed the Monarchy in the person of Victor Emanuel. To begin with it all seems incredible. What induced this Republican to make Victor Emanuel King of Italy? Look it up in history and you will find that without Garibaldi there would have been no Italian Monarchy. And then again, Garibaldi is associated with other personalities—Cavour, Mazzini—whose outlooks and leanings are poles apart from his own inner attitude. Cavour and Mazzini are men of utterly different mentality. Mazzini, the idealist who takes no part in practical affairs; Garibaldi, invariably the practical, militaristic statesman but for all that seeming to hover a little above the earthly; Cavour, the shrewd, astute politician—how do these men fit together? That was the problem. And precisely here something comes to light that I will put before you as a characteristic feature in karma. It turns out that these other three men had been followers of Garibaldi when he had been an Initiate in Hibernia; they were his pupils. Now it was an essential principle of the old Irish Mysteries that a vital link should be formed between pupil and teacher. They cannot separate from one another, at all events not in certain incarnations. A karmic tie is forged and there can be no separating. In this particular case we find very singular circumstances: about the year 1807, these four men are born again, one in Genoa, two in Turin, the fourth in Nice—that is to say in the same corner of the globe and also approximately at the same time. They are born together—in the same epoch and in the same region. This is a case where men who belong together are brought together again, in spite of their personal leanings. A fervent Republican such as Garibaldi is tied to Victor Emmanuel—a man with such different persuasions and convictions—and the human relationship counts for far more than all the rest. I give this example to show you what human relationships that are based on karma, really signify. The one may believe this, the other that—but the karmic connection is by far the stronger bond. It is these human relationships that take effect in life, not so much the abstract things mediated by the intellect. But it is only by examining karma in characteristic cases that we discover how human beings are connected with one another, and how, if they have shifted away from the stream to which their own karma really belongs, they may pass through life like shadows.

So much for to-day. We shall continue these studies to-morrow.

## *Lecture Six*

We will turn our attention to-day to manifestations of the life of soul able to lead us to a kind of self-observation in which a vista of our personal karma, our personal destiny, flashes into life like lightning. When we reflect upon the nature of the life of soul even with more or less superficial self-knowledge, we realise that sense-impressions and the thoughts we form about them are the only clear and definite experiences in the life of soul in which, with ordinary consciousness, we are completely awake. As well as these thoughts, sense-impressions, sense-perceptions, we also have, of course, the life of feeling. But just think how indeterminately our feelings surge through us, how little we can speak of inner, wideawake clarity in connection with our life of feeling. Anyone who faces these facts with an open mind will certainly admit that as compared with thoughts, his feelings are indeterminate, lacking in definition. True, the life of feeling concerns us in a more intimate, personal way than does the life of thought, but for all that there is something undefined in it and also in the way it functions. We shall not so readily allow our thoughts to deviate from those of other people when it is a question of reflecting about something that is alleged to be true. We shall feel that our thoughts, our sense-impressions must somehow tally with those of others. With our feelings it is different. We allow ourselves the right to feel in a more intimate, more personal way. And if we compare feelings with dreams, we shall say: dreams arise from the night-life, feelings from the depths of soul into the light of day-consciousness. But again, in respect of their pictures, feelings are as indeterminate as dreams. Anyone who makes the comparison, even with such dreams as enter quite distinctly into his consciousness, will realise that their lack of definition is just as great as that of feelings. Therefore we can say: it is only in our sense-impressions and thoughts that we are really awake; in our feelings we dream—even during waking life. In ordinary waking life, too, our feelings make us into dreamers.

And still more so the will! When we say: 'Now I am going to do this, or that'—how much of the subsequent process is actually in our consciousness? Suppose I want to take hold of something. The mental picture comes first, then this picture completely fades away and in my ordinary consciousness I know nothing of how the impulse contained in the 'I want' finds its way into my nerves, into my muscles, into my bones. When I conceive the idea, 'I want to get hold of the clock', does my ordinary consciousness know anything at all of how this impulse penetrates into my arm which then reaches out for the clock? It is only through another sense-impression, another mental picture, that I perceive what has actually happened. With my ordinary consciousness I sleep through what has happened intermediately, just as in the night I sleep through what I experience in the spiritual world. I am as unconscious of the one as of the other. In waking life, therefore, there are three different and distinct states of consciousness. In the activity of thinking we are awake, completely awake; in the activity of feeling we dream; in the activity of willing we are asleep. We are in a state of perpetual sleep as far as the essential core of the will is concerned, for it lies deep, deep down in the region of the subconscious.

Now there is something that in waking life too, is always rising up from the depths of the soul, namely, remembrance, memory. When we contact immediate reality, we have thoughts. This immediate reality makes a definite impression upon us. But the *past* of this earthly life plays all the time into present reality in the form of thoughts and memories, of recollected thoughts. As you know, these recollected thoughts are much dimmer, much less distinct than the impressions of present reality. Nevertheless they do well up and make their way into ordinary waking life. And when we give memory free play, letting it recall all that we have passed through in life, we realise: here is our own life of soul, rising up once again. We feel that in this earthly life we *are* that which we can remember. Think only what becomes of a man who cannot remember some period of his life, whose memory of that period is completely obliterated. We may come across such cases and I will give just one example.—There was a man in a respectable position who while his life was pursuing its normal course, remembered his past, what he had done in childhood and during his education, what he had experienced as a student, and then in his profession. But one day his memory was suddenly blotted out. He no longer knew who he was.—I am telling you of an actual case.—Strangely enough it was not the reasoning faculty, not the mental grasp of immediate reality that failed; the *memory* was completely blotted out. The man no longer knew who he was as a boy, as a youth, as a grown-up; his mind could grasp only what was making an impression upon him at the moment. And because he no longer knew who he was in boyhood, youth or maturity, he could not link his present with his past life; this was impossible from the moment his memory faded.

A case like this makes it easy for us to realise just *why* we do one thing or another at a particular time; it is not because of the pressure of immediate circumstances but because of certain experiences we have had in the past—primarily in the past of our earthly life. Just think of all that you might do or leave undone if memory played no part in your actions! Man is dependent upon memory to a far greater extent than he imagines. The misfortune that befell the man of whom I told you, was that after the sudden obliteration of his memory he was guided only by the impulses of the present moment, not by any promptings of memory. He put on his outdoor clothes and left his home and family. He was tied to them only through memory—and now this memory was blotted out. Impulses worked in him that had nothing whatever to do with memories of his family. His reason and intelligence remained; and so—because it would have been senseless to do these things while other people were there—

he waited until they happened to be absent. He had lived with his family as a sensible, rational individual, but his memory had gone. He went to the railway station and took a ticket for a place a long way off. His mind was absolutely clear in a matter where reason came into play. He got into the train and went off; but the *memory* of what had happened, even the memory of having taken the ticket was blotted out. He was aware only of the immediate present. The extinction of memory was a pathological condition. But he was so intensely engrossed with the present that he knew when he had arrived at his destination; he could compare this with the timetable. The ability to read—something that had already become habit and was therefore no longer a matter of memory—that too had remained. He alighted and took another ticket to a distant destination. And so he went on, travelling about the world without knowing who he was. One day his memory returned, but he knew nothing of what he had been doing since buying the first railway ticket. When his memory returned and he was himself again, he found himself in a Casual Ward in Berlin. It was only the things that had happened in the trains and the places where he had been that were blotted out, for they did not belong to the present. Just think what a state of confusion! How utterly uncertain of himself such a man must be! You will realise from this how closely our 'I', our Ego, is bound up with our store of memories. We know nothing of the self within us if we are bereft of the store of memories.

What is the nature of these memories? Memories are of the nature of *soul.* But in the whole range of man's life and being they are present in another form as well. They work *purely* as soul-forces only in a human being who has reached the age of twenty one or twenty two, and continues living. Before then the memories do not work purely as forces of soul. We must be very conscious of what I have said in these lectures, namely that during the first seven years of earthly existence our physical corporality is an inheritance from our parents. At the change of teeth it is not only the first, milk teeth that are expelled—that is only the final act; the whole of the first body is discarded. We build up the second body—the body we bear until the onset of puberty—out of the soul-and-spirit we brought with us when we came down from the spiritual world to physical existence on the Earth. But from birth until the change of teeth we have received a host of impressions from the environment. Our being was absorbed in what flowed into us through having learnt to *speak*. Think of all the wonders that stream into us together with the power of speech! Any unprejudiced observer will agree in this respect with the statement made by Jean Paul to the effect that he had learnt more in the first three years of his life than in the three academic years. The meaning of this is clear. For even if the academic years are extended to five or six—not, presumably, because one learns too much but because one learns too little—even if this period is considerably extended we learn only the merest trifle in comparison with what we assimilate during the first three years of life, and thereafter through the years following the first three until the change of teeth. After a certain time all this remains in the form of hazy, indefinite memory. But just think how pale and indistinct are these memories of our first seven years compared with the events of later life. Just try to make the comparison. The memories often seem to loom up like erratic boulders without any obvious connection. And why? What we take in during the first seven years of life and what we take in later on have entirely different tasks to fulfil. What we take in during the first seven years works with intense activity at the plastic moulding of the brain, passes into the very organism. There is a great difference between the relatively undeveloped brain we possess when we come into earthly existence and the beautifully developed brain that is ours by the time of the change of teeth. And the result of this work penetrates from the brain into the whole of the rest of the body. This inner artist we bring with us from pre-earthly existence works in a most wonderful way upon our physical body during the first seven years of life. It is miraculous to see the facial expression, the look, the mobility of the features, the purposeful movements of arms and limbs beginning to appear in a child after the lack of definition characterising early babyhood. We see how spirit begins to permeate the child's being and the impressions he absorbs. The way in which spirit permeates the child during the first seven years of life is one of the most wonderful sights imaginable. When we observe how the physiognomy and gestures of the child develop from birth until the change of teeth, when we read and decipher it all just as we decipher something in a book from the single letters, when we know how to connect the forms of the gestures and the facial expressions appearing in succession just as we can connect the letters of a word and so *read* the word—then we are gazing at the workings of the brain which has been kindled into activity by the impressions received; these can form themselves only into sparse and scattered memories, because the plastic development of the brain and therewith of the physiognomy has primarily to be provided for.

As life continues its course from the time of the change of teeth to the onset of puberty, the forces working in this way are more or less lost to sight. As I said, until the beginning of the twenty-first year, work continues upon the shaping and elaboration of the organism; but from the seventh year onwards this work is less concerned with the *bodily* nature—and still less from puberty until the beginning of the twenties. But something else comes to our help. If we have any aptitude for this kind of observation and mellow it by contemplating the marvellous phenomenon of the child's physiognomy which reveals itself month by month, year by year in greater clarity, above all if we can perceive what the child's gestures reveal, how the awkward, unskilful movements of the limbs turn in a most wonderful way into movements filled with intelligence and purpose—this sensitive perception can be deepened and finer organs of sense will develop. Then, when we have before us a child between the ages of seven and fourteen, that is to say between the second dentition and puberty, when the changes in the physiognomy and the gestures are less marked and the development less obvious, it is possible through inner feeling which has all the certainty of an eye of soul to perceive how the child's development is proceeding in a more hidden way. And from this delicate, intimate observation of the bodily development of a child between the seventh and fourteenth years, there can arise the faculty to gaze into the life preceding the descent to earthly existence, the life between death and a new birth.

These things must again be within our reach, enabling us to affirm of a child between the ages of seven and fourteen: around you there is not only the sense-world of nature; in everything that is revealed in sense-perceptions, in colours, in forms, lives the spirit! It is truly wonderful to see the spirit becoming articulate in all things and then, as it were in a mirror-image, to perceive a reflection of this in the way in which spirituality reveals itself more and more distinctly in the physiognomy of a child. If we feel this deeply and inwardly and with a certain reverence make the experience a living power in the soul, then, as we observe the child between the ages of seven and fourteen, this reverence will lead to an understanding of how the pre-earthly existence of a human being between death and a new birth works into him here on Earth. And we shall feel that this bodily development is governed, not by the forces of the earthly environment but by the second physical organism which we ourselves mould according to the model provided by the first.

This can be of great importance in life. Humanity will have to learn to perceive the essential nature of Man. Life will then undergo the deepening without which the further progress of civilisation is simply no longer possible. Our civilisation has become totally abstract! In our ordinary consciousness we are no longer able to think in the real sense; we can only think what has been inculcated into us. We are no longer capable of perceptions as delicate as those of which I have been speaking. Hence men to-day pass each other by in ignorance. They learn a great deal about animals, plants, minerals, but nothing whatever about the subtle, impalpable processes of the development of the human being. The whole life of soul must become more intimate, more delicate, purer, and then we shall again perceive something of the real nature of human development itself; and this will lead us eventually to a vista of pre-earthly existence.

Next comes the period immediately following puberty, the period between the onset of puberty and the twenty-first or twenty-second year. Just think of all that a human being reveals to us in this phase of his life! Even with our ordinary consciousness we see evidence of a complete change in his life, but it takes a crude form. We speak of the hobbledehoy years, of the 'awkward' years and this in itself indicates our awareness that a change is taking place. What is actually happening is that the *inner* being is now emerging more clearly. But if we can acquire sensitive perception of the first two life-periods, what emerges after puberty will appear as a 'second man', actually as a second man, who becomes visible through the physical man standing there before us. And what expresses itself in the awkwardness, but also in very much that is admirable, appears like a second, cloudlike man within the physical man. It is important to detect this second, shadowy being, for questions on the subject are being asked on all sides to-day. But our civilisation gives no answer.

The turn of the nineteenth/twentieth century was accompanied by momentous changes in the spiritual and physical evolution of the Earth. Men of the ancient East had divined this and said that Kali Yuga, the Age of Darkness, would come to an end at the close of the nineteenth century when an Age of Light would begin. This Age of Light has begun in very truth but men are still unaware of it because in their minds they are still living in the nineteenth century and their ideas flow on lethargically. Nevertheless around us there is clear, radiant light and if we pay heed to what will reveal itself from the spiritual world, we can become aware of this light. And because youth is peculiarly sensitive, with the turn of the century an undefined longing arose in the hearts of the young for a more intimate knowledge, a much more intimate perception of Man. Human beings born about this time—at the turn of the nineteenth century—have the instinctive feeling: we need to know a great deal more about

Man than people are able to tell us. Nobody tells us what we long to know! There was this striving, this urgent, insistent striving for an understanding of Man. Children and young people were ill at ease with their elders for they longed to hear from them something about Man, and these elders knew nothing. Modern civilisation can say nothing, knows nothing about the spirit of Man. But in earlier epochs people were able, speaking with real warmth of heart, to tell the young very much about Man. When thoughts were still quick with life, the old had a very great deal to say—but now they knew nothing. And so there came an urge to run, run no matter where, in order to learn something about Man. The young became wanderers, path-finders; they ran away from people who had nothing to tell them, seeking here, there and everywhere for something that could tell them something about Man.

There you have the real origin of the Youth Movement of the twentieth century. What is this Youth Movement really seeking? It is seeking to find the reality of this second, cloud-like man who comes into evidence after puberty and who is actually there within the human being. The Youth Movement wants to be educated in a way that will enable it to apprehend this second man.—But who is this second man? What does he actually represent? What is it that emerges as it were from this human body in which one has observed the gradual maturing of physiognomy and gesture, in connection with which one is also able to feel how in the second period of life from the change of teeth to puberty, pre-earthly existence is coming to definite expression? What is making its appearance here, like a stranger? What is it that now comes forth when, after puberty, the human being begins to be conscious of his own freedom, when he turns to other individuals, seeking to form bonds with them out of an inner impulse which neither he nor the others can explain but which underlies this very definite urge. Who is this 'second man?' He is the being who lived in the earlier incarnation and is now making his way like a shadow, into this present earthly life. From what breaks in upon human life so mysteriously at about the age of puberty, mankind will gradually learn to take account of karma. At the time of life when a human being becomes capable of propagating his kind, impulses to which he gave expression in earlier earthly lives also make their appearance in him. But a great deal must happen in human hearts and feelings before there can be any clear recognition, any clear perception of what I have just been describing to you.

Think of the great difference there is in the ordinary consciousness between self-love and love of others. People know well what self-love is, for every individual holds himself in high esteem—of that there is no doubt! Self-love is present even in those who imagine that they are entirely free from it. There are very few indeed—and a close investigation of karma would be called for in such cases—who would dream of saying that they have no self-love in them. Love of others is rather more difficult to fathom. Such love *may* of course be absolutely genuine, but it is very often coloured by an element of self-love. We may love another human being because he does something for us, because he is by our side; we love him for many reasons closely connected with self-love. Nevertheless there *is* such a thing as selfless love and it is within our reach. We can learn little by little to expel from love every vestige of self-interest, and then we come to know what it means to give ourselves to others in the true and real sense. It is from this self-giving, this giving of ourselves to others, this selfless love, that we can kindle the feeling that must arise if we are to glimpse earlier earthly lives. Suppose you are a person who was born, let us say, in the year 1881; you are alive now; once upon a time, in an earlier earthly life, you were born, say, in the year 737 and died in 799. The man, personality B, is living, now, in the nineteenth/twentieth century; formerly this personality—you yourself—lived in the eighth century. The two personalities are linked by the life stretching between death and the new birth. But before even so much as an inkling can come to you of the personality who lived in the eighth century, you must be capable of loving your own self exactly as if you were loving another human being. For although the being who lived in the eighth century is there within you, he is really a stranger, exactly as another person may be a stranger to you now. You must be able to relate yourself to your preceding incarnation in the way you relate yourself now to some other human being; otherwise no inkling of the earlier incarnation is possible. Neither will you be able to form an objective conception of what appears in a human being after puberty as a second, shadowy man. But love that is truly selfless becomes a power of knowledge, and when love of self becomes so completely objective that a man can observe himself exactly as he observes other human beings, this is the means whereby a vista of earlier earthly lives will disclose itself—at first as a kind of dim inkling. This experience must be combined with the kind of observation I have been describing, whereby we become aware of the essential, fundamental nature of man. The urge to apprehend the truth of repeated earthly lives has been present in humanity since the end of Kali Yuga and is already unmistakably evident. The only reason why people do not speak about it is because it is not sufficiently clear or defined. But let us suppose that a thoroughly sincere member of the modern Youth Movement were to wake up one morning and for a quarter of an hour be vividly conscious of what he had experienced during sleep—and suppose one were to ask him during this quarter of an hour: what is it that you are really seeking?—he would answer: 'I am striving to apprehend the *whole* man, the being who has passed through many earthly lives. I am striving to know what it is within me that has come from earlier stages of existence. But you know nothing about it; you have nothing to tell me!'

In human hearts to-day there is a longing to understand karma. Therefore this is the time when the impulse must be given to study history in the way I have illustrated by certain examples; it is this kind of study which, if earnestly and actively pursued, will lead human beings to an understanding of their own lives in the light of reincarnation and karma. That is why in these lectures I am combining studies of historical personages with indications that will gradually lead to perception of man's own individual karma. By the time we come to the last lecture we shall have gained a clear idea of how man can begin to glimpse his own karma. But the only way to achieve this is to observe things first of all in the great setting and structure of world-history. The primary aim of this lecture was to shed light on the inner nature and being of man and it has also been possible to elucidate the inner aspect of the strivings of a promising Movement of the times.—And now let me conclude with a picture drawn from world-history.

Study of history in the future must be concerned with the *whole* man, must realise that man himself carries over from one epoch into the next the impulses that work in history, in the development of world-history. Let us think of the days when Charlemagne was reigning in Europe—it was from 768 to 814 A.D. Just recall for a moment everything you know about Charlemagne and what he accomplished. As so much about him is taught in school, I am sure that countless details will come into the minds of my listeners! At the same time as Charlemagne, a very important personage was living in the East, namely, Haroun al Raschid. He was a product of the scholarship associated in those days with Mohammedanism and he was fired with the will to foster and promote this oriental scholarship at a centre of learning and culture. Extraordinary results were achieved at his Court, for the highest attainments of the physical sciences, of astronomy, alchemy, chemistry, geography, as they were in those days, converged, so to speak, in him. Art, literature, history, pedagogy—all these branches of culture flourished at the Court of Haroun al Raschid. When one can perceive what was actually accomplished at this Court, the spectacle is far grander, far more impressive than that of the achievements of Charlemagne's Court, above all in respect of spiritual culture. Moreover there is a great deal in the campaigns of Charlemagne that the modern mind will not exactly admire! Living at the Court of Haroun al Raschid was another personality, one who in those days was simply a very wise man, but who in a much earlier incarnation, a long time previously, had been an Initiate. I have told you that the results of Initiation in an earlier incarnation may recede into the background in a later epoch. A most wonderful academy was established over in the East at that time and this other personality of whom I am speaking possessed real genius as an organiser. Scholarship, art, poetry, architecture, sculpture, the sciences—all were organised and brought together by this man at the Court of Haroun al Raschid. Both Haroun al Raschid and his wise Counsellor passed in due course through the gate of death and their evolution proceeded. This was the time when Arabism was spreading over Europe. The spread of Arabism came to a halt, but Haroun al Raschid himself, as well as his Counsellor, continued to be associated with its influence. Whereas the gaze of Haroun al Raschid in his life between death and rebirth was directed to Arabism as it swept through the North of Africa, across to Spain and further upwards to Western Europe, the attention of the other, the wise Counsellor, was directed from the East across the regions North of the Black Sea and from thence towards Middle Europe. It is strange that in following the life of a man between death and a new birth, one can also follow those things upon which his gaze is directed as he looks downwards. As I have told you, what he is actually beholding are the deeds of the Seraphim, Cherubim and Thrones whose workings are connected with what is happening on the Earth. In the life between death and a new birth we look downwards to the Earth, just as on the Earth we look upwards to the Heavens. The work of these two souls continued long after the close of their physical lives. Outwardly, they were reborn as men of very different characters. Haroun al Raschid appeared again as *Lord Bacon of Verulam*, the originator of the modern scientific mentality. Those who are capable of unprejudiced observation can see in everything that was forced upon the world by Bacon, a new edition of what was once cultivated over in the East. In the East men had turned away from Christianity. Bacon was outwardly a Christian, but inwardly, in his real aims, unchristian. The other man, the one who had once been the wise Counsellor, followed the path which led across to Middle Europe via the regions North of the Black Sea. It was he who as *Amos Comenius* brought Arabism over in a quite different form—a much deeper, more inward form than that in which it was introduced by Bacon—but who did, nevertheless, bear Arabism into the modern age.

And so at the dawn of modern spiritual life, two streams intermingled. We can perceive this development of history quite clearly—it is a phase when Christianity is temporarily forgotten, when on the one side scientific culture is externalised, but on the other becomes all the more inward. In his incarnation which had its roots in the East and then ran its course amid the deeper spiritual life of Middle Europe, much of the Eastern element persisted. It is not by casually opening some book . . . in a certain dialect there is an expression '*ochsen*' (to 'swot') and I can think of no other word at the moment . . . and then swotting up Bacon and Amos Comenius, that we can discern the inner evolution of the human race; we must rather begin to perceive how the development of the several epochs is brought about by *men themselves*, how the impulses are carried over from earlier into later times. Try for a moment to picture quite clearly what happened here. Christianity has spread, has taken a certain hold in the regions of Middle and Northern Europe. But through men like Bacon of Verulam, the reincarnated Haroun al Raschid, and Amos Comenius, the reincarnated Counsellor, something creeps in that is not genuine Christianity, but merges nevertheless with all that is working like so many spiritual streams in world-evolution. Only in this way is it possible to grasp what is really happening and to understand the great world-processes in which man is rooted.

If we go back to the time preceding Haroun al Raschid, to a man who was an immediate disciple of Mohammed, we must be quite clear about what it was that had been indoctrinated into oriental spiritual life through Mohammedanism.

Study of original Christianity reveals the deep significance of the fact that it has the *Trinity*. When we think of the Spiritual in nature, the Spiritual Power which places us in the world as physical human beings and operates in the laws of nature, namely, the *Father Being*, we may ask ourselves: What should we be if the Father Being alone worked in us? Through the whole of life, from birth till death, we should be under the same sway of necessity as prevails in the world around us. But in point of fact, at a certain age in life we become free beings, not in any way losing our manhood but awakening to a higher form of it. The principle that is working in us when we attain our freedom, when we release ourselves altogether from the sway of nature, this principle is the Son Being, the Christ—the Second Form of the Godhead. But it is the Power of the Holy Spirit that quickens within us the recognition that we live not in the body alone but having been associated with the body through its phases of development, we awaken, we are awakened as beings of Spirit. Man in the fullness of his being can be understood only through the Trinity; it is there that we perceive the concrete reality. But over against the Trinity, Mohammedanism proclaims an abstraction: There is no other Divine Being save the Father God, the one and only God. The Father is all; it is not lawful to speak of a threefold Godhead. In Mohammed himself, and in his followers, this doctrine of the one Father God was personified.

In an epoch when the highest human faculty capable of development was that of thinking in cold, barren abstractions, when men knew only the one, abstract God, they began more and more to identify this God with thinking, to deify the life of thought and the human intellect—forgetting that real thinking has an essentially *altruistic* tendency. In Mohammed's followers, this talent for thinking about the world in pure abstractions was expressed with a certain originality and grandeur. One of these followers was Muawija. I wish you could look him up in history. You would find there a strange mental configuration, the prototype, as it were, of men who think in pure abstractions, who want to shape the world according to tenets contained in a few simple paragraphs. Muawija, one of Mohammed's followers, appeared again in our time as *Woodrow Wilson.* A revival of the abstract thinking of Mohammedanism gave rise to the view that it is possible to shape a whole world by applying the principles set forth in fourteen prosaic, abstract paragraphs, void of any real substance. Truth to tell, there has been no greater illusion than this in all world-history; no other illusion has proved such a pitfall for wellnigh the whole of mankind. Before the war, when I spoke in the Helsingfors Lecture Course* of Woodrow Wilson's shortcomings—his fame was then just beginning—people were unwilling to understand when over and over again, wherever I had the opportunity of speaking, I indicated that the calamity looming ahead was by no means unconnected with the idolisation of Woodrow Wilson then going on in the world. Now, since the impulse of our Christmas Foundation, the time has come when such things will be spoken of openly and without reserve, when our studies of history will also be connected with matters that are potent impulses at this very time. Esotericism must permeate the whole Anthroposophical Movement in order that what lies hidden beneath the shroud of external history may be brought into the light of day. Men will not be equal to the task of coping with world-events nor of doing what needs to be done until they begin to study karma and until individuals learn to observe their own being, as well as world-history, in the light of karma.

* *The Occult Foundations of the Bhagavad Gita.* 28th May–5th June, 1913.

## *Lecture Seven*

We are all the time coming nearer to an understanding of those elements in the lives of individuals that can give us an inkling of the place of karma in their personal existence. In order to reach this goal in the course of these lectures it will be my task to-day to indicate how karma can be investigated by Initiation-science, to begin with through actual experience of karma, and how man—at first without Initiation-science but with a certain intimate capacity for observing life—can develop insight into the potency of karma. Let us remember here what I have said about memory and thoughts which stream up in their multitudes from the depths of the world of soul, some summoned by our own activity, some rising up freely. They are thoughts which give us a picture, shadowy and more or less abstract it is true, but for all that a picture of our earthly life since birth. Attention has recently been drawn to what a man loses if he loses his memory. He is then still able to act quite sensibly and reasonably, but he does not act out of the context of his whole life; he acts as if at the point of time when his action begins he remembers nothing of his life hitherto; he acts, in fact, as if he had come into the world as a skilful, intelligent, rational individual but as if his life hitherto had simply not been spent on this Earth. From this we see how for the ordinary-level consciousness of to-day, the Ego is anchored, grounded, in the memory but in the case referred to can no longer find its bearings along the path of memory leading through this earthly life.

But what does this memory amount to? Let us compare it with the actual experience of the reality from which the memory comes to us. We have our place in life, we go through life with its joys and sorrows, find ourselves interwoven in our experiences with the whole of our being. But just compare the intensity of feeling that accompanies an actual experience with the shadowy remembrance preserved in the soul. We need only take an especially significant event in life, for instance, the death of a friend who was particularly dear to us, or the death of father or mother, at a time when such a happening would be an exceptionally deep experience. Let us compare the full intensity of the event and the moment when it was experienced, with the shadowy memories that come to us ten years later! And yet we must have these shadowy memories in order to be aware of the continuity, the intrinsic value and reality of our Ego in earthly life. But is it not evident from this how the Ego, which can find no bearings in earthly life without memory, really experiences itself in a shadowy way, how it is anchored in what actually sinks down every night into unconsciousness? As a matter of fact we do not experience our 'I', our Ego, with very great intensity in ordinary-level consciousness on Earth. The real Ego of life that is not immediately present grows more and more akin to thought, although we know that it is connected with the Ego of to-day. Experience of the present has intensity but this intensity is absent from experiences that have become remembrance. So that we can say: (a drawing was made) if *this* is our perceptive soul, our spirit, which are in living intercourse with all that streams in upon us from the outside world, behind this Ego we experience in shadowy recollection what remains to us of it. The characteristic feature of this memory is that feeling and also impulses of will are more and more sifted out of it. However intense our feelings may have been on the occasions referred to, the death of someone extraordinarily dear to us, for instance, yet the memory picture which remains has become dim, more and more devoid of feeling. And even less is there any continuance of what we then undertook out of our will-impulses under the impression of the moment! Feeling and will fade away; the calm memory-picture, a mere shadow of what we actually experience, is all that remains as a rule. And we can exist in the land of Earth only if this shadow of an experience remains with us. Our relation to memory is one thing, to present experience quite another.

But we can approach direct experience in another way, not as we usually do; we can ask new questions about our experiences. It must be admitted that if we look back on life it assumes a remarkable aspect. Let us ask ourselves what we really are at the present moment with our knowledge, with the quality of our feeling, the energy of our will. And if we return to our experiences with these newly asked questions, we shall discover how poor we should be, after having reached a certain age in life, if our previous experiences had not been there! If we look back, more particularly to many experiences of youth and relate the remembrance of them to the present day—how happy they were! If we often look back over our life we can say to ourselves something highly significant for the present moment. We can say: we owe the facility with which we adapt our soul, perhaps even our physical constitution with more or less dexterity to life, to the circumstances that in youth we were able to live happily, not suffering from depression, that we were led to much that gave us joy. These impressions of joy in the soul endow us in later life with a certain happiness, although it is drawn down into deeper regions of our being. Let us now ask how much of what life brings us in the way of inner deepening, how much of this is to be attributed to our sorrows, our sufferings? And let us also ask: what can arise in the soul if we look at our life with these questions in mind? We must give the answer to these questions not with the intellect, but with feeling. And feeling answers: I must be thankful to all that has come into my life because only thereby have I become the being I am and with whom I more or less identify myself. I cannot know whether otherwise I might have been of even less account. I can only be thankful to life, because I have become what I am through its joys and sorrows.

This question must be answered with a feeling of thankfulness to life. And it means a great deal if this thankfulness for earthly existence finds its way into the human soul. If certain deepenings of the soul are achieved and life is judged not out of emotion but out of the soul in its purity, then this thankfulness always arises. Though much of what life has brought us may be deplored, yet in many respects the regret is the expression of a complete error. For if what is regretted had not taken place we should not be what we actually are. The feeling that we can have about life amounts ultimately to this thankfulness. Thankfulness may also be felt even when we are not entirely in agreement with life, when we would like to have had more from our existence. We can also be thankful if we are given a small cake by someone from whom we might have expected the present of a large one. The fact that we had expected a large cake must certainly not weaken our thankfulness. And so it can truly be said that whatever, in our opinion, life has denied us—and this opinion may after all be erroneous—it has at all events brought us something. For what it has brought us we must develop the feeling of thankfulness. But when in all earnestness we develop the feeling of thankfulness—we need only reflect on this and it will be readily understood—there must be thankfulness for something else. Anyone who has developed thankfulness to life will be led, through this thankfulness itself, to recognition of the invisible spiritual Bestowers of life and to the transformation of memory in loving devotion to them.

The most beautiful way for one's personality to be led to the supersensible is when the path leads through thankfulness to life. Thankfulness is also a way into the supersensible and finally it becomes veneration and love for the life-bestowing spirit of man. Thankfulness gives birth to love and when love is born from thankfulness to life it opens the heart to the spiritual Powers permeating all existence. And as life began with our birth and we cannot possibly begin to be thankful to life merely from our birth as we then already obviously possessed certain qualities, it is therefore quite certain that thankfulness to life leads out of this life into pre-natal existence. In order to be fully aware of what I am now saying it must in any case be proved in actual life. If thankfulness develops out of unprejudiced observation of life, let us test whether love that quickens insight into the spirit is not actually born from this thankfulness, and we shall find that it is so. The question arising here can indeed only be answered through life itself, but life answers as I have indicated. When, however, through actual experiences we develop thankfulness and love to the life-bestowing spiritual Powers our feeling is quite different from anything associated with memory. We *experience* vividly, with intensity; in memory our experiences become pale shadows. Memory owes its existence to our experiences; but we now come to something that is mightier than our ordinary Ego.

When we consider the experiences that have come to us we are not concerned merely with our shadowy memories; we are concerned with something mighty, not with the shadow of our Ego flowing through time, but with the creator of this earthly Ego. Outside on every hand are the events to which we owe our existence, and when we consider these events we must acknowledge them to be powerful creators of our earthly Ego. We stand in the middle of them with our momentary, present Ego; behind us, if we look into our soul, are shadowy after-images of our experiences; before us, there is weaving destiny, the successive experiences of destiny which have formed and moulded our Ego. The transition from thinking to feeling belongs in fact to this vivid feeling of the shaping of destiny, for thankfulness and love can be experienced only in the realm of feeling. It is to this thankfulness and love that there comes a presentiment of an irrevocable destiny. When we have divined the existence of this ruling destiny, having experienced thankfulness and love, we begin to feel the power of the events that have made us what we are. Think of someone of forty years of age: he has made his mark. In order to take an extreme example, let us say that he has become a great poet—after all there have been such people! . . . I might also say, not to go far afield, a noted physiologist, or physicist, but I will take an imaginary example. This man looks back to his eighteenth year; he goes through the events from his fortieth back to his eighteenth year and finds that at the age of eighteen he failed in his leaving examination. At that time it had been a great grief to him. But he had been obliged to arrange his life differently, for he had not enough money to repeat the year, or to go through the wide world as a student who had failed in his examination. Everything was already prepared! Had he passed the examination he would have become an excellent financial inspector, have done an immense amount of work, but have had no time to develop the facilities and powers lying in the underground of his soul. Of course it can be said that if these powers of phantasy exist they are so strong that in any case they would break through the financial activities! This can be said in the abstract, and is invariably said, but it is not true. Many a poet owes his special temperament and what he has become to the circumstance that something of the nature I have indicated happened to him. He will be grateful—if he sets any value on having become a famous poet—to the examiners who 'failed' him and did not hinder the course of his life by giving him 'excellent' in each subject. Whatever life has been, when we take it in its reality and not sentimentally we can certainly develop this thankfulness and acknowledge that we have been forged by the destiny that goes with us or against us. But at all events we must undergo this feeling in order to see destiny as it were weaving as living reality before us.

Here I should like to interpolate how the same experiences come to one who possesses Initiation-knowledge, one who can therefore see into the spiritual world. He directs his gaze—which has already been sharpened by the Imaginative and Inspired knowledge he possesses and about which you can read in the book *Knowledge of the Higher Worlds*—he directs his gaze to some particular experience. One who has intensified and strengthened his knowledge can direct his gaze with particular intensity to any experience he is undergoing at the present moment. If a man has Initiation-knowledge he is affected by the experience not less but more strongly than if he has no such knowledge. From the fact that he apparently undergoes experiences with much greater composure than a man who has not this knowledge it must not be concluded that he is less deeply moved by them. He is much more strongly affected than the other. It is only that he has acquired the power to look with composure and objectively at the hard experiences of life; deep down in his being he feels them more significantly than does the other. So when a man endowed with Imagination and Inspiration has experiences they are intense and strong; and because he has practised the relevant exercises in this and in the preceding life he can transform the experiences into pictures full of content, into actual Imaginations.

In what does this transformation consist? It consists in the fact that not only does what the eyes see of the events and experiences, stand there, but that the deeper spiritual connections become evident and a picture which is also carried about with one when the experience has passed, arises; the experience has passed but the picture is immediately present. The experience is intense and through Imagination the spiritual connections play into it. The soul is strongly stirred and it is then possible to look into the spiritual reality and to retain the experience. If a night goes by, the experience, which has become more intense because the astral body and the Ego go out of the physical body, is carried into the spiritual world. What has been experienced in the physical world with the physical and etheric bodies together can be experienced in the spiritual world only with the Ego and astral body; but then, on waking, it is driven back again into the physical body. But it is not brought back as if by the ordinary consciousness which is restricted to memory which gradually fades away. It is carried back in such a way that one's whole being is permeated as with a phantom; it is carried with one in full objectivity, in all intensity, and it resounds with the reality of another human being standing bodily before one.

And then again two or three days or nights pass. Then, after these two or three days or nights the following happens: what was first carried into the spiritual world by the Ego and astral body and has been brought back so that it is quickened and vibrates in the physical body, yes, even becomes articulate and stands behind the experiences as the ruling destiny. The experiences are not alone; they are now coloured by what produced them in former earthly lives, by the forecast of how they will go on working in the earthly lives to come. Just as we put memory as a shadowy image behind us, one who has Initiation-knowledge puts experiences in front of him so that they are clearly there before him. But they become as transparent as glass and behind them, like a mighty cosmic memory, stands the evolving karma, the objectivised memory. And one becomes aware that man not only has within him the shadowy memories of earthly life but that his karma is engraved around him in the cosmic ether, the Akashic Chronicle. Within is shadowy memory, without is the cosmic memory of our destiny through the lives on Earth even although it remains unknown to the ordinary-level consciousness.

Our passage through the world may be sketched like this (a sketch was made). We walk over the ground of the Earth bearing within us shadowy memories. If we were to picture to ourselves a human being with these shadowy memories in him we should have to picture them as a little cloud in the region of his head—where the head passes over into the body—gradually becoming more and more shadowy towards the body. As a human being moves through the world he is surrounded by an etheric aura in which all his experiences are inscribed but also everything that is inscribed in him from the previous earthly life. We have an inner memory and we have the world's memory outside us. Every human being is surrounded by this aura. Not only is the present life engraved in us by way of memory, but round about us the earthly lives of man are engraved. It is not always easy to decipher this memory, but it is there. The deciphering is difficult and in the instances of which I have spoken to you during the last few days, the deciphering was not easy to convert into knowledge. But everything is *there*. Man has not only a memory within him but an auric memory around him. It is not possible in a single moment to call up a remembrance of what one has passed through in life. The remembering always requires several days. Here, waking up and going to sleep must also come into play, as I have described. It can never be said that as some experience has been undergone one should necessarily remember how it was affected by earlier lives on Earth. It must be fixed in the mind clearly and imaginatively, permeated with inspiration; and then one must wait until it reveals itself. One must never speculate about the spiritual world in research, never invent anything, but only make the preparations for enabling something to reveal itself from the spiritual world. Anyone who believes he can force the spiritual world to reveal this or that to him will be very greatly mistaken; nothing but errors will come of it. Preparation must be made for what one may hope to receive out of the spiritual world more or less by grace.

Such is the path of knowledge which with Initiation-science can reveal karma. It reveals that each human being bears karma as a kind of aura around him. But through the path of thankfulness in life I have described it is possible to have an inkling of the karma a man carries around him in this way. This inkling of being enclosed in a karmic-auric mantle can come to one. It will take more than a period of a few days as would be possible with Initiation-knowledge, but it will come about gradually in the course of more intimate self-observation—often with respect to experiences lying in the far past, to which we turn our gaze. But if a certain event of our past life is mature enough for us to recognise that the forces of preparation in earlier earthly lives are playing into it, then we certainly have an inkling of the truth. Unfortunately, however, it is rare to-day for a man to penetrate so deeply into his own soul that he achieves this grasp of his own experiences or even comes near to developing the feeling of thankfulness. People to-day take life far too externally. They rush through life without pausing quietly to realise the nature of their various experiences. If one has grown up with a certain perception of the cosmic significance of human life, it may sometimes seem quite remarkable how far individuals are from being what they imagine themselves to be, how often they are simply borne along by life without making any strong individual impression.

Here too I should like to speak of concrete cases. I once came across a history teacher, who was a very clever man and also gave his pupils this impression. It might be said that when he chose to do so he lectured with a certain inner enthusiasm which lent emphasis to his words and when the right moment came, enthusiasm for him as a teacher was aroused in his pupils. There was something remarkable about him. I saw him at the time when he could arouse real enthusiasm among his pupils. But then life got the better of him; he became slack, and the enthusiasm that formerly permeated his lectures was no longer there. He read aloud from books, supposing that the pupils did not know them and would not come across them. But one day a pupil went up to the rostrum and saw the book from which he had been reading, whereupon all the pupils bought it, learnt its contents thoroughly and became excellent scholars. At last he became so superficial that he no longer knew what he was telling the pupils in his class. This transformation came about in a relatively short time, and one could not help being amazed to see how ineffectual he was after having quite recently been able to generate such enthusiasm. A few more years went by and the same teacher of whom I once heard a number of pupils say with the characteristic enthusiasm of youth: 'There's a man for you! He is really enthusiastic about history . . . one can learn something from him!'—this man ended quite remarkably, in a life of stagnation and triviality. In a few years he had degenerated to such an extent that he was obliged to live outside the town where he had been a teacher; he was so little respected that it was impossible for him to live in the town.

Such a change for the worse in destiny seems a great riddle and if life is taken earnestly enough it is through such cases that one begins to ask questions about karma.

For very many other human beings seem to jog along in the same old groove, undergoing no such radical changes. To genuine spiritual knowledge such destinies as the one of which I have told you become great problems. Through spiritual knowledge we are led on the one hand to the great problems which in the lecture yesterday, at the end of a series of incarnations, brought us to Woodrow Wilson, but on the other hand, in the life immediately surrounding us we are led in thought to the great questions of human destiny. If we observe an example of this kind quite without prejudice we make the discovery that surely it cannot have its origin in the present life! And there will be countless other, quite different cases, where no such twists of destiny take place. We must therefore set to work with the strong desire to understand such questions of destiny. And other cases arise. I will give another example. These examples always seem to me to have been placed in my own path in order to give my conception of karma the right colouring.

I also came to know another man personally—also a teacher. He was even more revered than the one of whom I have spoken, quite extraordinarily revered by his pupils. They believed him to be the greatest sage at present existing in the world. This was the impression made upon his numerous pupils—not upon all, not, for instance, upon myself, but that is a personal matter and is not characteristic. And now a most remarkable thing happened. One could have believed from the relation of this man to his pupils—he had thrown himself into his teaching with all enthusiasm, with every fibre of his soul—that it apparently satisfied him. Yet one suddenly discovered that he was extremely glad not to be obliged to teach any longer; he had been appointed Director of a much less important school than the one in which he had formerly taught. He was delighted to be able to carry out the business of Director which was much more trivial work than actual teaching. And the most striking and surprising thing of all was that this same man, who could speak inspiringly about Homer and Aeschylus, who presented geography in a wonderful way to his pupils, that this same man ended in trivial party-political circles. It was absolutely incomprehensible!

I am bringing this forward only as an example for I could add any number more to the two cases of which I have spoken. They would be personalities about whom one has the feeling that their Ego has been little affected by life. They stand there as personalities upon whom life has little effect; it has touched them externally only. If it touched them when they were still near their training-college examination or during their University training when they listened with enthusiasm, then they were full of zest. If life has led them to trivialities, then they accommodate themselves to the trivial, and are contented too; nothing touches their souls at all deeply. If it were a matter of cleverness, of intelligence . . . well, how many people would be Anthroposophists to-day! Millions of individuals to-day are clever enough to grasp Anthroposophy. What hinders them in our time from coming to Anthroposophy is that in their souls they take life superficially, letting life flow past in its depths, its superficialities, its banalities. They can be unimportant school-reformers for a time and after that sit all day in cafés and play billiards, without a single pause from morning until night. Such things do indeed go on in our modern life.

Here the great question arises as to why this happens. In the case of many souls it becomes apparent in what a remarkable way such circumstances have come about. A whole number of personalities such as those described through the two examples, lead one back into the early Christian centuries, when they had their most important previous incarnations. One is led to those centuries when in the South and also already to some extent in Middle Europe, Christianity had assumed the form which later on it has still in many ways retained. It was a time when, as I have shown in the book *Christianity as Mystical Fact*, the Mystery-wisdom out of which Christianity had grown, had faded away. The Mystery-wisdom had contained the experience of the Cosmic Christ, the knowledge that the

Christ had proceeded from the Sun, which is a spiritual reality in the Cosmos, and had come to the Earth in order to be for the Earth that which He has indeed become. This knowledge which extends from the Earth into realms of cosmic spirituality existed among influential Christians in the first century and faded away in the fourth, fifth, sixth and seventh centuries A.D. Then it faded away so thoroughly that to-day it has come to the point—but it began at that time—when the strongest rebuke levelled against the conception of Christ held by Anthroposophy is that Anthroposophy regards Christ as a Cosmic Being, as a Sun Being. Everywhere among our opponents it is accounted to be Anthroposophy's greatest crime that it has a cosmological conception of Christ. It is said that this is a warming-up of what once existed as Gnostic Christianity. —Now people have no idea whatever of what Gnostic Christianity is. For with the exception of a few fragments such as the Pistis Sophia, from which little can be learnt, the Gnosis has become known to posterity only through the writings of its opponents. Hence nothing is really known about it. And now think about this question: if nothing were to remain known of Anthroposophy except the writings of my present opponents, if everything were destroyed except their writings—what would be said about Anthroposophy in times to come? Many critics endeavour to treat the numerous anthroposophical books in existence as the Gnostic writings were treated. If these critics were to succeed, nothing would remain except the writings of opponents. It would be to them that people would turn in the first place—to purely antagonistic literature! That would be extremely interesting! External research into the Gnosis had nothing to go on except the writings of opponents! So it is simply nonsense to talk about the ancient Gnosis having been raked up, for nobody could do such a thing without knowledge of the Gnosis derived from its authentic writings, but these have been lost! It cannot be understood from works mostly written by opponents and nothing else has come down to posterity. But even so, to connect the Christ with the Spirit of the Cosmos is accounted to be the greatest sin. In any real conception of the Gospels, every page, every sentence points to the cosmic nature of Christ. But that conception has gradually been rooted out. And it was at the time when the Gnosis had been most thoroughly exterminated that those individuals who when they come again to-day do not get to grips with life, were for the most part incarnated. In that previous incarnation, when they were already clever and intelligent the culture of the age prevented them from knowing anything about the Earth's connection with the spiritual life in the Cosmos. It was because they stumbled, as it were, through life, thinking of the Earth as enclosed in itself with nothing but physical stars to be seen outside that in the next incarnation they can only turn to meet the impacts of real life with stumbling steps.

And so we look into the destiny of men. We discover that the culture of the age exercised this influence upon a very large number of human beings, that it made them superficial and they come to the present incarnation already with the tendency to superficiality as I have described to you. For that is how you experience these men, who once, in an earlier incarnation lost connection with the spirit-powers in the Cosmos; in the incarnation following the decisive one referred to, they cannot find the connection with earthly life. But thoughts about karma must do more than introduce mere reflections into our life, they must bring *will*, activity. We must therefore bear constantly in mind: How will it be in the future, if to the inability to grasp the Spirit in the Cosmos is added the inability to grasp earthly life, if men's attitude to the trivialities of life is no different from their attitude to the deep realities of life? Then indeed the study of karma becomes a serious matter. It can thrive among us only if pursued with the greatest earnestness.

My wish to-day was to consider karma more from the aspect of feeling.

## *Lecture Eight*

From many studies on the subject of the forming of human destiny or karma you will have realised that human life is not viewed in its entirety if sleep is left out of consideration. When a man reflects about himself with the ordinary consciousness of to-day, he looks back only upon the days because the nights are passed in unconsciousness. In the case of normal sleepers, therefore—as nowadays there are no Seven Sleepers—a third of life is disregarded. But for experience of the supersensible and of man's participation in the spiritual world, it is this very third of life that is of essential importance. When a person has reached a definite age he looks back over the days he remembers, as far back as his memory goes. The nights are between the days but in his recollection the nights are left entirely out of consideration. A true retrospect is really not possible for a man of modern times because his observation of life is far too superficial. But if he were capable of carrying out such a retrospect, then precisely through what he does *not* see in the ordinary way he would have an indication of karma. Observation of the life of sleep gives significant hints of individual karma. Attention must above all be paid to the essential difference between the two moments of waking and going to sleep.

Ordinary consciousness can feel this difference instinctively, but Initiation-Science alone can throw light upon it. The difference between the moment of waking and the moment of going to sleep is particularly evident to people who are sick or ailing. They notice more readily than do those in good health that the moment of going to sleep is often accompanied by at least a slight feeling of pleasure. The moment of waking, on the other hand, has something slightly unpleasant about it; waking is accompanied by happiness only if the attention of the person concerned is at once turned to the outer world and when his consciousness of the outer world drowns what is rising up from within him. For many people the moments both of waking and of going to sleep are shrouded in a certain dimness. At the moment of going to sleep a man has the feeling that he is somehow dragging the past day's experiences along with him, that these become more and more nebulous and that he then abandons them. The moment of waking is accompanied by a slight feeling of oppression, a feeling of lifting oneself out of certain depths, bringing from them something that is carried over into the day and is got rid of only during the course of it. The result is that a certain feeling of unpleasantness may be associated with the experience of waking. An unpleasant sensation of taste may intensify into an equally unpleasant sensation of a stupefied head. People do not as a rule distinguish between these delicate experiences but they are unmistakeable indications of a great deal in human life. For what is really taking place? We describe quite correctly and from a certain standpoint very exactly what is taking place if we say: during sleep the physical and etheric bodies lie in the bed and the ego and astral body pass out into the spiritual world, returning into the physical and etheric bodies in the morning on waking. But how does this process take place? In order to make progress in our study of karma we will envisage the whole process which, to begin with, it is justifiable to describe in a rather abstract way.

This emergence of the ego and astral body from the physical and etheric bodies can be sketched like this.

Let us suppose this figure to be the human being and here are the physical body and the etheric body. In the evening, when sleep begins, the ego and astral body move outwards. We will draw quite diagrammatically how the two members widen out, expand, but describe a kind of circle. In the morning, on waking, the ego and the astral body pass into the physical body again through the limbs, actually by way of the fingers and toes. The fact is that a circle is

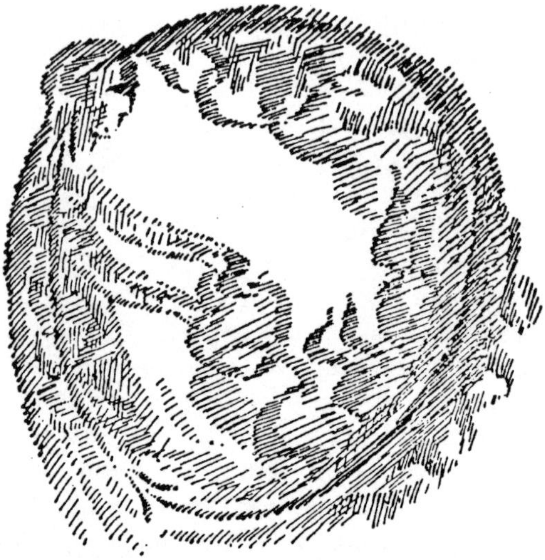

described and this statement must be taken more literally than is usually imagined. In reality, when a normal human being wakes in the morning, the picture seen by clairvoyance is not of the whole astral body and the whole ego being immediately within the physical and etheric bodies; on the contrary, ego and astral body pass only slowly and by degrees into the physical body from morning onwards until towards midday and afternoon. You will say that if this were really the case we should feel our ego and astral body moving only gradually from the tips of the fingers and toes towards the head. To very exact clairvoyant observation this is actually the case, only the person concerned does not inwardly feel it to be so, for the reason that the way in which these higher principles work is different from any kind of physical activity. You see, if a locomotive is propelling a carriage, it pushes forwards from the spot where it is at the moment. And if a railway line is, say 30 metres long and the engine is pushing forward, as long is needed for the first metre, then so long for the second, and so on, at a certain point there may be no effect from the engine if it has not yet reached thus far. But with spiritual conditions it is different; spiritual conditions are effective at other places as well as where they happen to be centred. So the waking hours of the day are used for the purpose of bringing our ego and astral body slowly into our physical and etheric bodies from the tips of our fingers and toes. But the ego and astral body begin to be active from the very beginning, from the moment of waking, so that one has the feeling of being completely filled by them. To clairvoyant sight, however, it is clear that an actual revolution takes place through the day; the complementary revolution takes place during the night. But a revolution also takes place—one that is less dependent upon time—when you have an afternoon nap. Here again the ego and astral body leave the physical and etheric bodies and the process adapts itself to your need of sleep. Sleep is a prophet and knows when you will wake although you yourself do not; your astral body under all circumstances knows it. It knows when you will wake even if as the result of some disturbance you sleep for a shorter time than you intend, even if before going to sleep you say that you want to sleep for only half-an-hour but you lie asleep for three hours instead. The astral body knows exactly how long you will sleep. It is an accurate prophet because the inner, spiritual circumstances are, in fact, different from the external circumstances experienced at the time.

You will certainly have realised that there is a very great difference between the process of going to sleep and that of waking. When we wake we have just been in the spiritual world and when we go to sleep we pass out of the physical world and into the spiritual world. A stream bears us along in the spiritual world between sleeping and waking and we also have experiences then—experiences which are, however, wrapt in unconsciousness. We have experiences during sleep which are, in fact, similar to those of the daytime, only they are of much greater intensity.

If you observe the soul's waking life you will find there, in the first place, the thought-experiences evoked by the

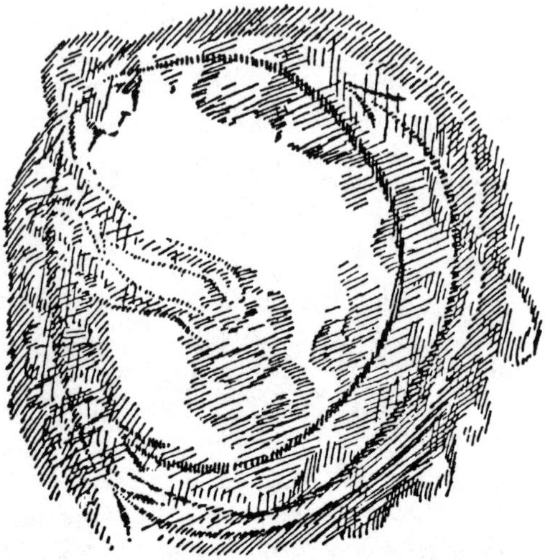

various impressions made by life. But memories of the earthly life already past are always intermingled with these experiences. Try for once to consider how in every situation memories mingle with the momentary impressions made by life. In fact, if close attention is paid, one can get a picture of how, at different moments, life is a veritable hotch-potch, a mingling of memories and instantaneous impressions. There are two quite different factors: the thoughts which rise up from within and the thoughts which enter via the senses. These are quite different currents of the inner life and during sleep they are also in evidence. The stream of what is present (impressions of the daily life) on going to sleep continues during the night and perpetually flowing towards this is what we experience on waking.

These two currents stream towards each other: the one stream, experienced particularly on going to sleep, is the one already mentioned, the one that is experienced consciously, vividly and powerfully during the first decades after death when life is lived through again in reverse order. As I put it to you rather drastically: if you give someone a box on the ear, then, in living through the event after death you do not experience the anger which you consciously felt on Earth when giving the blow, or maybe the satisfaction at being able to express the anger. Instead, you undergo what the other person experienced, *his* physical pain and also *his* moral suffering. This is what you would experience, but in a picture, not yet in reality, if you could consciously continue your life when it is already becoming dim at the approach of sleep. If you were to pass into sleep with full, clear consciousness, you would live through the day's experiences in reverse, but in pictures. Whereas during the first decades after death it is all experienced as *reality*.

What I have described applies, approximately, to life by day in the waking state, when we are given up to outer life merely with our thoughts. But there is also the other current and this has something stupendous in it. We experience it on waking, as I have explained, but there is an element of heaviness in it which is carried into the day and is only gradually overcome; later in the day we become free of it. When this second stream is fully perceptible to Initiation vision it is seen to be a repository of the whole karmic past which passes before the human being every time he sleeps. Whereas a person can experience something of the karma that is taking shape for the future, when he wakes from sleep he has in the feeling I have described a faint, admittedly a very faint, glimpse of his present karma. The moment of waking brings a faint indication of what an individual bears within him from his past earthly lives. This is of course taken into what the astral body and the ego radiate when from the tips of the fingers and toes they spread through the body. A very burdensome karma, a karma that is difficult to bear, radiates unhealthy material deposits into the head, whereas a good karma radiates health-bringing deposits. And it is here that the spiritual and the natural make contact. The good in a man's karma radiates the healthy states of the organism into the head in the morning and clarifies it; healthy elements radiate upwards from good karma. From bad karma, from the residue of whatever guilt has been incurred, unhealthy deposits in the human organism are reduced to a kind of vapour which rises up into the head. The head then feels dull and heavy. The weaving of karma right into the physical can be perceived from the condition prevailing on waking in the morning. Karma takes shape through the alternating effects of sleeping and waking life. Now just as the karma that takes shape from what we have done every day of our life until its end, signifies in sleep during the night what the momentarily formed thoughts signify during the day, so does that mighty spectacle encountered when we have slept from evening to morning signify the *cosmic memories* of our past karma. Just as we have personal memories when we wake, from going to sleep until waking we have our karmic memories, if our consciousness extends so far. Memories of the different lives through which we have passed on Earth come to meet us. Soon after going to sleep there can be revealed to one who is able to understand such experiences through Initiation wisdom and Initiation insight, the last Earth-life, the last Earth-life but one and so on, right back to lives which become indefinite because the individual himself was then still living in the universal All, with a dreamlike, plant-like consciousness. Thus sleep is actually the window through which man looks at his karma. He becomes familiar with his karma and works at its further shaping during sleep through the deeds and thoughts which fill his waking life. This is the first weaving of karma: it takes place during sleep. We have already considered a second weaving that takes place during the first decades after death.

We shall acquire a more serious conception of life when the significance of sleep has been grasped in this way, when we realise that we sink into sleep every night because it is then that we work at the formation of our karma, and because it is during sleep that our karma from previous earthly lives finds the way whereby it can play a part in our daily life. From the night, karma gradually enters into our daily life and we bring something quite definite with us into the day. An individual who can recollect clearly how at one point in his life a particularly significant event occurred to him, will, if he has a more intimate, finely developed faculty of introspection, easily perceive that if, let us say, this event took place in the afternoon, ever since morning an inner restlessness was impelling him towards it. Most people who can perceive something of the sort will have had the feeling that from the morning onwards they had been moving towards an event that was to be significant in their life. Such an event—if it was a really fateful although entirely unexpected event—affected all the preceding hours of the day. On days when something important is to happen to us we do not wake up exactly as we do on days that take their usual course—only we do not notice it. Those who used to lead the life of peasants on the land—such people knew about these things and did not like to be torn suddenly out of sleep, because when there is no gradual transition into the waking life of day one is wrested away from such intimate experiences. Peasants say that on waking one should never look at the window at once but away from it, so that while the light is still dim one can become aware of what is emerging from sleep. The peasant will not at once look at the window nor does he like to be startled into waking suddenly; he likes to be wakened naturally, at the same time every morning by the church bell, so that he can prepare himself for this through the whole period of sleep. Then the day dawns, the church bell sounds into his life and then, in the early morning he has inklings of his destiny, of events of destiny, not those resulting from acts of free will. This is what he likes to happen and unlike people claiming to be highly civilised he would hate to be wakened by an alarum clock, for that drives one with dead certainty away from everything spiritual—much more forcibly, of course, than the window looked at immediately on waking. But our modern culture has introduced materialism into all the circumstances of life and will continue to do so. There is a great deal in modern life which makes it impossible for men to perceive the spirit living and weaving in the world. The more aware they become of that indefinite, half mystical influence which can radiate from sleep, the more clearly is their attention directed to their karma.

And now you will understand why I was able to say that we readily dream of individuals whom we meet in life and to whom we at once feel drawn or the reverse, quite independently of whatever outer impression they make. What is happening in such cases? These are individuals with whom we were together in earlier lives on Earth. Let us say that in the afternoon of 14th June, 1924, we have had the experience of meeting someone we perhaps dislike. We now carry into sleep the experience that gave rise to the feeling of dislike. But there, in sleep, the karma is revealed; this person stands before us as he was in the last earthly life or in the last but one, and so on; we meet him as he was in his earlier life. We encounter everything we experienced in connection with this individual who has now appeared and who simply reminded us of something—we meet him as a bodily figure, but in a spiritual way. No wonder that we begin to dream of him; with ordinary consciousness we cannot do otherwise. But if we come across an individual for the first time, however beautiful or ugly his features may be or however strongly he interests us, in our sleep we never meet him, for he was never with us in earlier lives on Earth. No wonder we cannot dream of him! You see how transparent such things become when he facts are examined spiritually.

Now what transpires between sleeping and waking in the forming of karma may follow a normal, perfectly normal course. Then a man will experience how his destiny takes shape as the fulfilment of what he brought upon himself in earlier earthly lives. Or he will experience the ultimate karmic value of what he thinks or does in this present life. It will as a rule live itself out in what he thinks or does. But something quite different may come about.

Suppose a man who is living on the Earth today achieved in deed or thought something of real importance in an earlier life. The karmic result of this does not lie in the physical body or in the etheric body which are inherited from the parents, but it lies in the astral body and ego—

the members which are outside the physical and etheric bodies during sleep at night. But suppose that this karmic load has such strength that it cannot wait until the age of life when the astral body may be weak, for in old age muscles and bones have already become brittle. Let us take seventy years—the patriarchal age—to be the normal length of a man's life on Earth. In these seventy years man's astral body and ego also undergo development. The astral body of a child can work strongly and forcefully upon the whole physical and etheric organism; it can hammer, as it were, upon muscles and bones. In old age this is no longer possible, for the astral body then becomes relatively weak. The strength of the ego increases but it withdraws into the weaker astral body and hence works with less power. The astral body, however, is particularly responsible here, for in old age it is no longer able to hammer effectively upon muscles and bones. Now imagine that someone is living at the present time, in the twentieth century, having lived before in the fourteenth or eleventh century. During his life in the eleventh century he performed a really significant act, one that made very strong impressions on the astral body. The ensuing result remains in the astral body and when the man comes again in the twentieth century it wants to be finally fulfilled and from this astral body to give the necessary stimulus. When the result of the experience in the eleventh century is of such significance that it cannot make use of a feeble, aged astral body hardly capable of performing important deeds, then it must use an astral body in the early years of life. And if the event has been so important as to eclipse all other events of life, a great deal must be compressed into the period while the astral body is still youthful. What does this mean? It means that the individual concerned will have a *short* life in the twentieth-century incarnation. Here you see how the length of life is determined by the consequences of former earthly thoughts and deeds being anchored in the astral body.

We now go further. Think, for instance, of an astral body that is positively inflated as the result of important deeds—

particularly evil deeds—in an earlier incarnation; such deeds inflate the astral body and it makes a strong impact upon the physical and etheric bodies. This strong impact is not healthy; only a certain normal relation of the astral body to the physical and etheric bodies is healthy. The strong impact which can, for instance, be caused by bad karma, batters the organs, softens them and causes disease. Now comes the second incarnation. Such action or thinking in the eleventh century can inflate the astral body, thereby condemning the individual to death at an early age. But he may fall ill in any case, apart from this violent impact; he may have a severe illness and die from it. That is the physical aspect. For when we see what is going on in the person's physical body, we say: he is ill and the illness ends in death; he falls ill at the age of twenty-five and dies at thirty in consequence of the illness.

Is this also the spiritual aspect? Is this also what would be said by Initiation Science? No! Initiation Science would say the opposite. For it is precisely the earlier significant action or thought that brings about the death in the next earthly life; the deed in the eleventh century brings about the death in the twentieth century. And the death sends the illness on in advance . . . a man becomes ill so that he may die at the right moment. The consequence of the later death, which is a karmic necessity, is, as you now realise, the illness which is sent in advance. That is the spiritual aspect. When one rises from the physical world to the spiritual world everything is in fact reversed; it takes the opposite course and we see how the illness is karmically brought into man. That is the karmic aspect of illness. This karmic aspect of illness can be an extremely important factor for diagnosis. It need not immediately be discussed with the patient but it may certainly be important. If you bear in mind that what is contained in karma has its own definite place, you will certainly discover it.

Now if the significant incident, action or thought affecting another human being or some particular matter occurred in an immediately preceding incarnation, let us say in the

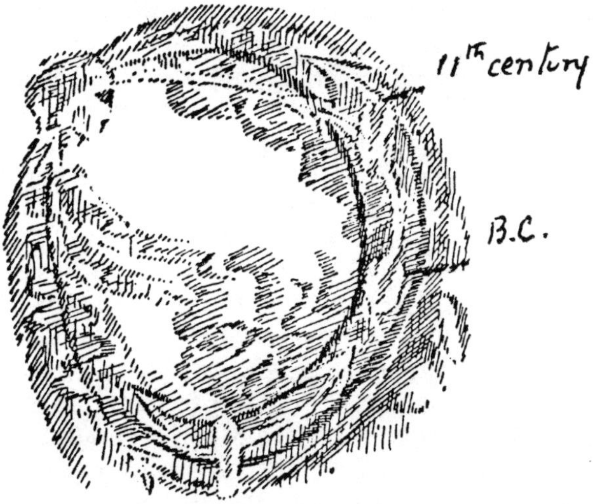


eleventh century, when we are asleep we encounter what took place in that century before anything dating from a still earlier incarnation, let us say in the second century B.C. Thus we gradually encounter what has happened to us in earlier earthly lives. But if one begins *here* (pointing to the sketch) then what is encountered first is what has made the way from here to here. The karma comes to meet us; but this means that what is above here has come from what is below, perhaps from the heart; something that is low down in the organism and was affected in the previous incarnation comes, however, from the head. In the case of illness, therefore, when we see how far back the influential events lie, karma can indicate to us that an affection, let us say, of the legs, comes from incarnations in the relatively near past, whereas a symptom of illness in the head comes from incarnations in the relatively far distant past. Thus the transition from the spiritual into the physical can also be indicated by karma.

What results from this is extremely important for therapy. For where must we seek the remedy for illness affecting the head and for illness affecting the legs? The remedy for illness affecting the head will be found in what existed far, far back in the evolutionary process of Nature, in what is reminiscent of very early Nature-processes, for instance, mushrooms, which in their present imperfect form recapitulate an earlier plant formation, or in algae and lichens, or, in the case of the fully developed plant, in the root, since that is the part that has remained at the earliest stage. Illness in the lower body and more towards its periphery will have to be healed with what appeared at a later stage in the evolution of Nature, namely, blossoms, flowering plants or also with later formations in the mineral kingdom. Whatever is a late development in man must be healed with what is also a late development in Nature. In the head, too, there are, of course, organs which are comparatively late formations. When the Earth was still recapitulating the Moon-evolution and Sun-evolution, man existed without his present eyes, in general without sense-organs, although the first rudiments of them were already present during the Saturn-evolution. As they are today, mirroring the outer world inwardly, they are a relatively late product of evolution, appearing at the same time, for instance, as silicious substance in its present form on the Earth. Silica as it is today is a late product in the evolution of the world of Nature, although its rudiments were laid in the far, far past.

Hence when silicic acid is correctly administered as a remedy it acts upon everything belonging to the nerves-and-senses system, especially the senses, through the whole organism. In their present form the senses developed in an age when rocks containing silica also appeared in their present form. In the first incarnation which can still be called an incarnation, when with our whole bodily make-up we were a more integral part of Nature, we lived, simply in accordance with our karma, an existence shared with different forms of plant and animal life, the successors of which are here to-day. The mushrooms and the roots of plants are unlike what they were in that early epoch but in a certain way what is present to-day in the mushrooms, lichens, algae and roots of plants is reminiscent of the conditions prevailing in our first definite incarnation. In the blossoms and flowering plants of today and in minerals at a corresponding stage . . . (a gap in the transcript here). I bring this before you only to show how a true observation of karma leads to stages in the evolution of Nature. And from the relation of Nature to Man we can recognise how to heal. Every branch of life must ultimately be widened in such a way that it gradually becomes spiritual knowledge. Everything else is so much groping and fumbling, an existence in spiritual darkness, and it is this that has brought mankind into the present situation. If men are to emerge from it again they must grasp the reason for it in clear consciousness, that is to say, knowledge of the physical must be widened to knowledge of the spiritual. And nothing can lead more positively to realisation of the spiritual than the study of karma.

When we picture how the forming of karma proceeds from sleep, how again it passes into and through sleep, how the normal forming of karma impels a man to action, makes his action again subject to karma and how he thus lives out the ordinary karma of life—from all this we see how karma works. When again we see how the life of an individual is shortened and he dies at an early age, indicating that karma has inflated his astral body and must make strong demands upon it as the result of past deeds, thus contributing to illness—everywhere the working of karma is in evidence. Or let us suppose a man has an accident and is ill as a result; then, under certain circumstances, such an accident—which is possibly, but not necessarily, determined by karma—can continue to be a factor in the further course of karma through the following lives on Earth. Illness may also be the *beginning* of karma and then it will be found that such illnesses make going to sleep an unwelcome and difficult process. But when illnesses are the beginning of karma they have something consoling about them.

In the case of many illnesses the following must be said: illnesses that are a fulfilment of karma, that make waking unpleasant, point to previous experiences; illnesses that are an augury of future karma and make going to sleep an unwelcome and difficult process are the beginning of good karma. For there will be compensation for what is suffered in such an illness. We have the pain now and afterwards the compensation for the pain, the uplifting, joyous experience. A great deal in life looks different when viewed from the spiritual and not from the physical standpoint. It is sometimes a thoroughly painful physical experience not to be able to sleep, but true observation of the spiritual aspect can be comforting. And if we do not value the momentary physical effect above the spiritual life we can actually say: Thank goodness that I so often have difficulty in going to sleep, for that is a sign that I shall experience much that will be uplifting in my future earthly life; a great deal from my present life will pass into the next one.

Sleeplessness can sometimes be a good comforter and if it were not karmically beneficial in its spiritual aspect, it would be much more harmful than it actually is. Many people tell one such legends about their long bouts of sleeplessness that from the medical point of view one might well ask how comes it that they are still alive! Normal sleep is essential for normal life. People tell one for how long they have not slept; one can only wonder that they are still alive for they really ought to be dead and yet they are not! But in such circumstances the vivifying spiritual element contained in the ego penetrates into life as compensation. To a brief survey of life it is obvious that really restful sleep after hard struggles and hard work is also at times desirable. But to lie in complete restfulness without sleeping and to pass the night quietly and fully awake is nevertheless the more desirable because when it is done of set purpose a person then becomes more and more aware of the Eternal. But the will must be in operation; the condition must not, in essentials at least, be due to physiological causes. Nevertheless there is karmic consolation for difficulty in going to sleep and in sleeplessness, for this really points to future karma, points to the future in certain respects.

# Lecture Nine

Let us compare what we learn through direct experiences about our relation to life between birth and death with what we must feel inwardly about the connection between our moral behaviour, thoughts and acts and the consequences of this behaviour. We began these evening lectures with just such studies and we will conclude with the same theme.

When on the one hand we consider how our moral deeds proceed from our purposes, from our whole attitude of soul, we realise that if we observe ourselves without prejudice, one category of our actions must be described as morally good, fit to become part of the world-order; the other category is of actions that must be described as morally bad, morally imperfect, unworthy to become part of the world-order. But whatever comes to pass through men cannot have a momentary significance only—this is admitted by everybody. And the same applies to the world of Nature. Everything has its effects, its consequences, becomes the cause of something or is itself the effect of something. Human life would certainly not be in keeping with the course of world events if what it embraces were not also cause and effect. But whereas we can be completely satisfied when we observe Nature and clearly perceive cause and effect, we certainly cannot be satisfied about the connection between our moral experiences and the course taken by the world-order. There appears to be no direct connection in the physical happenings between what ought to be the result of the moral disposition of our soul and what actually comes to pass in the course of physical life. And if we consider happenings in wider circles of people we see that a man who in respect of his soul-life seems to be morally good, encounters misfortune and evil in the world, while a man who seems inwardly weak and immoral may encounter external events that are in no way a requital for what is harboured in his soul. In short, we find no connection between what a man experiences as his destiny and the essential quality of his will. It could be called an irresponsible illusion if anyone were to deceive himself that in the one life on Earth the destiny he encounters is in any way the effect of his moral will. The bad can be fortunate, the good unfortunate. These two statements really summarise that characteristic of earthly life which makes it incomprehensible, to begin with, to human faculties. And we shall see from this that man, as he is now placed in the world, is himself not in a position to bring about the consequences answering to his deeds. In the single life on Earth morality remains an inner disposition, an inner attunement of the soul; it cannot become directly manifest in outer physical reality. Admittedly, the inner disposition of the soul can be a direct result of the moral attitude. We can be inwardly contented with our good conduct, in spite of being hit by misfortune that is in crass contrast to what we have actually done; but the experience brought about in this way remains in the realm of the soul. Man must acknowledge that in physical life he is not in a position to bring to outward manifestation in the world the inner, moral content of his soul.

When we study karma as we have been doing during the last few days, seeing how earlier lives work over into later incarnations, we realise that in the moral sphere of the life of soul the earlier is inwardly connected with the later. Put briefly, however, this means that here, in physical life on Earth, man has a constitution which forces back his moral conduct into the realm of soul, does not allow it to take effect in *one* earthly life. In a single earthly life man is powerless to give effect to the moral content he bears in his soul. His physical corporality, his etheric substantiality, make him powerless. In the life between death and a new birth, however, he becomes as powerful as here in physical life he is powerless. But if in his physical life the physical and etheric bodies render him powerless, there must be something in the life between death and a new birth that enables him to give effect to this soul-content, to make it a reality there, and physical reality too in later lives on Earth. On Earth we live in our physical and etheric bodies amid the kingdoms of Nature and it is what we have to take from Nature for these bodies that renders us powerless. With our own being of soul-and-spirit which passes through the gate of death we become powerful after death because we are then united with the Beings of the higher Hierarchies, just as on Earth we are united with the kingdoms of Nature. The Beings of the Hierarchies belong, as we know, to three realms: to the lowest realm belong the Archai, Archangeloi, Angeloi; to the middle realm belong Exousiai, Dynamis, Kyriotetes; to the highest realm belong Thrones, Cherubim, Seraphim. In the course of these lectures we have learnt how man lives between death and a new birth with the inmost essence of the stars and hence with these higher Hierarchies. But in order that the moral content of the soul may come to expression in life on Earth, the following must take place.

It is true that, to begin with, we have to retain in our soul the effects of our moral attitude of thought, feeling and will; we have to wait until in the life between death and a new birth we are vouchsafed the help of the Beings of the higher Hierarchies. What lies in our soul is first carried through the spiritual world, emerges again in a new earthly life and appears then in the form in which it is right to appear. For what should we be if in earthly life we could bring to direct fulfilment the moral content of our soul? We should not be typical men of terrestrial life! Just imagine that you bore within your soul a moral content that quite justifiably you considered could be capable of creating a favourable world-situation and that you could actually bring it about. What would you be then? You would be magicians, not typical men of the Earth! For when a power of spirit-and-soul is brought to direct expression, that is an essentially magical achievement. In our present cycle of existence man is no magician in the single life between birth and death. But he is a magician when, together with the Beings of the Hierarchies, he is active between death and a new birth and is able to continue these activities when he again descends into life on

Earth. The karmic development through these two entirely different modes of existence is in fact the process where the human being works magically. The physical human being standing before us in external life is membered—as I have shown at the end of the book *Von Seelenrätseln* (Riddles of the Soul)*—into the nerves-senses man, the rhythmic man and the metabolic-limb man. Metabolism and limbs are connected; when we use our limbs, metabolism is activated and must continue; forces in man must be used up. Metabolism must continue in inner experience too. But both are related. When we observe the human metabolic system as it operates in the physical body, we may be tempted at first to regard it as man's lowest system. There are people who claim to be idealists because they have accustomed themselves to look down with a certain superciliousness upon the metabolic-limb system. It is the lowest system, the system that the respectable idealist would prefer to be without. But without it earthly life would be impossible; it is the system that represents man in his imperfection in earthly life.

Now the facts of the matter are these. In the physical human form the metabolic-limb system is the lowest and therefore has little to do for what is essentially *human* in earthly life, but it is connected in this earthly life with the Beings of the highest Hierarchy, the Thrones, the Cherubim, the Seraphim. As we move about the world or work with our hands, in this mysterious activity the activity of the Thrones, Cherubim and Seraphim is present. These Beings remain helpers when man's life continues between death and a new birth. They remain helpers. Now it is quite erroneous to believe that the moral content of the soul proceeds from the head. In reality, regarded from a higher point of view, man's head is by no means such a tremendously important organ. The head is really more or less a mirror of the external world, and if we had the head alone we should know about nothing except the external world. The head simply reflects the external world. The experiences of the head are mirrorings,

* See *The Case for Anthroposophy*. Steiner/Barfield, (Rudolf Steiner Press).

reflections of the external world. Our inner, moral impulses do not proceed from the head but from the region of the metabolic-limb system, not, however, from the physical system but from its constitution of soul-and spirit wherein Thrones and Cherubim and Seraphim are living.

And so to acquire a right view of man we must picture the following.—(a drawing was made). This third member of man's constitution, the metabolic-limb system, seems at first to be imperfect, indeed it might be said that in respect of its physical and etheric organisation it is unworthy of the human being. But something else lies within it, or rather this system lies within something else; the Thrones live within it, the Cherubim weave within it, the Seraphim flame within it. When man passes through the gate of death, everything that underlies the physical metabolic-limb system falls away from him and with his ego he remains in the realm wherein he previously existed, namely in the realm of the Thrones, Cherubim and Seraphim. He then separates from them but they continue to develop the moral quality of the soul. Here on Earth man looks upwards, to the Heavens, in order to divine a higher reality, a spiritual-supersensible reality. He does this as long as he is on the Earth. If he is living between death and a new birth he looks downwards and beholds what the moral content of his soul becomes as a result of the deeds of the Cherubim, Seraphim and Thrones. There below, when he descends again to the Earth, the consequences are fulfilled; there the Cherubim, Seraphim and Thrones are working to bring about the fulfilment of the spiritual reality.

And so, after we have become attentive to it, we see how in a magical way man sends the consequences of his deeds of the present into the next earthly life.

Now that we have considered the metabolic-limb system, let us turn our attention to its polar opposite, the nerves-and-senses system. This, of course, extends through the whole organism but is established primarily in the head. We will therefore consider the human head. It is a fact that through the head man experiences only a reflection of the existing external world. His thoughts, his mental conceptions in which alone, as I have said, he is really awake, are actually only reflections from outside by way of the head. But when a man masters Initiation Science, at first through Imaginative knowledge, then, as you know, through its metamorphosis into knowledge through Inspiration and then through Intuition, he is able to look into his earlier lives on Earth—but he sees them then in their *spiritual* form. In the spiritual world, knowledge itself is reality. And the experience of a man who with genuine Initiation-knowledge is able to look into earlier earthly lives is that he is living not only, say, on June 15th, 1924, but is himself present through the course of the earlier lives; he not only looks into those earlier lives but he looks back upon his whole being. It is not abstract, theoretical observation but direct identification with his own former existence. His inner life is greatly stirred when he begins to experience his earlier earthly lives. But this experience makes it possible to change the focus of his world-outlook. What is the usual focus of a world-outlook? The usual focus is the head. This head with its physical organisation as the foundation, this head which was yours in previous earthly lives and in the immediately preceding life, cannot be made the focus of your world-outlook when you have once experienced earlier incarnations, for it has long since passed away. Only the spiritual principle that was present in the head can be made the focal starting-point of a world-outlook. Initiation therefore consists in this: through going back into his former existence on Earth, man spiritualises himself. All clairvoyance in the best sense of the word actually means going back into earlier earthly lives. To be initiated means not to remain within the limits of the present life but to look at the things of the world with the faculties that were ours in earlier earthly existence. Whereas in the ordinary course we are such imperfect beings in earthly life that we see only the external physical world, the beings we were in earlier existences had already become clairvoyant. And as a rule when we experience the immediately preceding incarnation we make the discovery that the person we were then was already much nearer perfection.

How does it come about that what we *could* have become after the earlier life has not been achieved? Why is this? You see, if as human beings having nothing but a head we were to pass from one earthly life to another, we should be as perfect in the later life as in the former, but we have the other systems as well as the head. And since the magical principle in man lies in the metabolic-limb system which in turn works in karma, karma brings the head across from one earthly life to another. Thus karma is directly active in the formation of the head. And if we begin to develop an unprejudiced view of man in this field, we shall gradually learn to read a great deal about his karma from the physiognomy of his head. To look at the human head with the ordinary consciousness of today is just the same as taking Goethe's *Faust* and beginning "I—h-a-v-e—s-t-u-d-i-e-d—a-l-a-s . . ." because then one knows only the letters and cannot read. When we have learnt to read we shall understand what these strange signs mean. As I said once before, this trivial fact brings it about that whereas we should otherwise see only about thirty different shapes of letters in books, we have Goethe's *Faust*, Hegel's *Logic*, the Bible, and so on, simply because we have learnt to read. In the same way we can learn to read the living things around us. The progress from merely spelling the form of the human head and *reading* it leads into the secrets of the karma of that particular person. As regards the outwardly perceptible form of the head we may say that every human being has his own particular head; no single individual has exactly the same shaped head as another. Although individuals often look alike, they are not alike in respect of their karma. In the head-formation the karma of a man's past is revealed to physical sense-perception. In the metabolic-limb system lies *future* karma; spiritually concealed, invisibly it is there. So that if we speak of man in the spiritual sense we can say: Man is so constituted that on the one hand he makes his past karma visible and on the other hand he bears his future karma invisibly within him.

In this way we can eventually acquire an inwardly spiritual

view of the human being. Man's metabolic-limb system is inferior in respect of its physical and etheric nature only, for in that system live the Beings of the highest Hierarchy. When we consider the physical-material aspect of the head it is undoubtedly the most perfect system because it bears within it, externally and visibly, what works over spiritually from earlier earthly lives. The head is generally the most highly valued, but it is not the most perfect in a spiritual respect. For whereas Thrones, Cherubim and Seraphim live in the metabolic-limb system, in the head-system live Archai, Archangeloi, Angeloi. It is they who stand behind everything we experience with our head in the physical world of sense. They live in us, in our head-system, and are active behind our consciousness; they encounter the effects of the physical world and mirror them back, and we become conscious only of the reflections. What we are aware of in our head-system is only the semblance of the activities of the Archai, Archangeloi and Angeloi. (A drawing was made). If I am to continue this diagram I must say: the Archai, Archangeloi and Angeloi are working, at the other pole, in the head-system.—I always use the nomenclature of the earlier Christian world-conception in which the spiritual connection was still intact, although the spiritual Beings may just as well be given other names.

Between the nerves-and-senses system which is based primarily in the head and the metabolic-limb system, man has the rhythmic system in which everything that is active between the lungs and the heart is contained. In all this activity live the Beings of the Hierarchy of the Exousiai, Dynamis, Kyriotetes.

In concluding our studies of karma we are led again to the realisation that while man faces the three kingdoms of Nature here on Earth, behind him are the spiritual kingdoms of the Hierarchies, one above the other. And as here on the Earth his physical body encompasses him and prevents him from bringing to fulfilment by magic the moral forces of his soul, after death the world of the Hierarchies receives him and enables him to make effective magically for the next incarnation what he cannot achieve in one earthly life. When a man passes over from one earthly life to the next he would in all circumstances, if his further evolution were to proceed consistently, develop clairvoyance with the head-system yielded by the former life; Archai, Archangeloi and Angeloi would lead him to clairvoyance. Hence if a man is to have insight into spiritual reality—insight that without an iota of superstition or charlatanry can be called clairvoyance—he must be able to project himself with a certain cosmic consciousness into his previous life on Earth, although in the external world he has progressed to his present incarnation.

Thus, if someone is living, let us say, in the twentieth century, he uses the body which this century can provide and for knowledge he must avail himself of the head. He cannot be clairvoyant. But let us suppose he were transported into a previous earthly life, say in the tenth or eleventh century, as the result of his meditative exercises now, in this twentieth century. He is not the same person as he was at that earlier time, but through his own forces he has brought it about spiritually that now, in the twentieth century, he is the man he was in that earlier epoch—a clairvoyant personality. Clairvoyance can reveal this clearly to Initiation-knowledge during life in the physical world. When we look closely into human life, however, it is revealed to clairvoyant consciousness that in the deeper impulses of a man's nature, in the deeper foundations of his soul, what was present in a former incarnation rises up again in a different form. It is therefore essential, if we wish to approach in earnest such matters as the working of karma, that earthly experience must be of a more spiritual character than is usual.

I will elaborate what I have been saying by means of an example. You know from the way in which I have given such examples that they are the findings of spiritual investigation undertaken with a deep sense of responsibility.

A certain individual lived in the European-Asiatic Orient, somewhat earlier than the founding of Christianity, with a task that was far from his liking. It was in an epoch when slavery was still prevalent and his task was to supervise a number of slaves belonging to a certain owner. Supersensible vision leads us to a situation where a human soul, incarnated at that time in the body of a slave-overseer, was obliged to carry out whatever the cruel owner of these slaves decreed. The slaves were in the care of the overseer and relationships of an ethical nature developed between them. But there was deep conflict in the soul of this overseer. It went against the grain to carry out the often cruel, disciplinary punishments ordered by his master. Nevertheless he obeyed, because he was accustomed to these circumstances and because it was natural at that time to act in such a way. Now just consider for a moment: are people to-day always what they would like to be? They do not often think about this; they deceive themselves about the disharmony between what they are and what they would like to be. This individual too was not what he would have liked to be, but intrinsically he had deep sympathy, deep love, for all the unhappy slaves upon whom he was obliged to inflict these cruelties. Social customs, so to say, caused him to hurt the slaves in many ways. He therefore shared the responsibility, although the master and owner of the slaves was primarily the culprit.

Both individualities were born again in the middle of the Middle Ages, and now as a married couple. The former slave-owner came again in a male incarnation, the overseer came as a woman. In the middle of the Middle Ages the reincarnated slave-owner held a position in a certain village commune, a position that was by no means pleasant, for he was a kind of police jailer and was held responsible for whatever happened in the commune; he felt that life was full of hardships. If we look for an explanation we find that these villagers were for the most part reincarnations of the slaves whom he had formerly owned and whom he had caused to be ill-treated by his overseer. The karmic result turned out to be that the former slave-owner, although he had become a fairly high official, was nevertheless the village jailer, who together with his wife was held responsible for whatever happened in the commune. But at the same time, because the wife shared in all the suffering that the one-time slaves caused her husband, the karma was fulfilled between her—the former overseer—and the slave-owner. The bond between these two was dissolved but not the tie between the one-time overseer, now incarnated as a woman, and the members of the commune. They came together again in the nineteenth century. The earlier overseer, who in a certain way had adjusted his relation to the former master, came again as the great educational reformer *Pestalozzi*, and those who had been the slaves under him were the children who received such infinite benefit from his educational principles.

These things must be viewed not merely with the prosaic intellect, but with soul, with feeling and with love which must become as clear and brilliant as the intellect and be able to develop genuine knowledge. The intellect can develop only pictures of outer Nature, and anyone who thinks that he gets something more than pictures deceives himself. It is possible to get more only if soul, feeling and love become forces of knowledge, and it is only by going back to earlier karma that we are gradually able to realise how karma works. But the whole soul must participate, and the content of these explanations of karma must be grasped by the whole being of man.

It really amounts to this: the soul must penetrate into the very essence of the Anthroposophical Movement. A short time ago I was deeply moved by a certain incident. What I have told you about Pestalozzi I had also said in a lecture in Dornach, and later on had occasion to visit an official in Basle, accompanied by another member of the Dornach Executive. The well-known picture of Pestalozzi among the children was hanging on the wall in the waiting-room. It was known to the member of the Vorstand who was with me. He was deeply moved by it and he said: When one looks at this faithful portrayal of Pestalozzi, one realises that such a situation can only have come about in the way that is revealed through Anthroposophy. This kind of thing is just what ought to occur more often, this realisation in direct experience of what has been discovered by anthroposophical investigations.

These indications of karma which I have now been able, to my great satisfaction, to give you, cannot make demands merely upon your intellect. What has been presented during these eight days calls not merely upon intellect but upon heart, upon the whole soul. And only when you have gathered together all that I have said about the reincarnation of historical personalities, about observation of individual karma, about the influences of sleeping and waking life in the development of karma and let it all work in your hearts and souls, will a comprehensive grasp of the working of karma in individual personalities result from these studies.

Our civilisation will be rescued from the grip of its present decline only if what is so readily taken to-day merely in an intellectualistic sense penetrates into the whole being of man. What does an Oriental say nowadays about Western man? The spirituality of an Oriental at the present time is not of a kind that we can adopt forthwith, but it is a spirituality which in the ancient past was able to gaze deeply into the supersensible worlds. To-day only traces have remained but in his soul an Oriental still has the feeling of what was once experienced in the East, namely, living communion with the spirit inherent in all things. Such is the experience of those who are not entirely steeped in materialism. One Oriental who had a feeling for the spirituality in Eastern wisdom said the following as he contemplated Western civilisation: 'Its essential characteristic is that it is only façade and has no foundations. The façade stands on the ground without any solid foundations.'—And this Oriental went on to say: 'Yes, in nearly everything that belongs to his civilisation, Western man actually starts from the standpoint of his ego, the ego that is enclosed within a single life and therefore has no reality. It has reality only when it emerges from its bounds and leads into the successive earthly lives'. Realisation of existence in successive earthly lives is regarded by the Oriental as the foundation-structure and remaining with the ego that is enclosed between birth and death he regards as the façade. Have we not heard to-day that when a man looks into spiritual reality he will look back into the past? If he contemplates karmic development with its magical processes he must have accepted the principle of successive incarnations. Then the ego widens out and will no longer be egotistic. The Oriental says that the European can recognise the ego only within the limits of birth and death and this he calls the egotism of the European. So he says that European, indeed Western civilisation as a whole, is only façade and has no foundation-structure; moreover that if this state of things continues and Western civilisation persists in recognising only the ego living between birth and death, the separate stones of the façade might one day fall apart as the façade has no foundation. This picture of the single stones crumbling away from the façade has actually arisen in many oriental souls, living as they do, largely in Imaginations. It is insight into such matters as have been studied here during these last few days that can add the foundation-structure and supplement the mere façade. Contemplation of the karma which reaches from earthly life to earthly life leads man beyond the restricted activity that is limited to a single life on Earth.

In what must be our final lecture, I should now like to place before your souls a vista into the cultural task of Anthroposophy. If it works on within you, revealing many things, you will become co-workers in the task of creating the foundation-structure for a true and genuine façade of Western civilisation. I have nothing to add to what has often been said by men of the East. What they really mean is this: the West has departed too far from the spirit, it can no longer find the foundation-structure; the East must contribute what it still possesses from ancient times in order that civilisation on Earth may not perish.

Whether this terrible fate that is prophesied for Western civilisation by all clear-sighted Orientals can be avoided, depends upon endeavours such as those of Anthroposophy. Resolute will is needed to penetrate into the spiritual world, in order that its forces may again be received into the hearts of men. Hence a community of human beings who have come together, as you have done, for spiritual activity, has grasped what this truly means only if the resolution is taken to apply all the forces of the will to the task of furthering, for the sake of humanity, experience of the spirit. My purpose in these lectures was to point the way to experience of spiritual reality and thus to the moral principle that is everywhere implicit in it. For this reason I wanted in these hours when we could be together again, to give you just what I have given. But in Anthroposophy spiritual things should be taken in earnest at all times, during every moment, not only during every lecture-hour. In Anthroposophy, therefore, it is true to say that when we are beside one another in space, we are together physically, but because we recognise spiritual reality we know that we are also together even when physically apart. And as I know that some of you here must travel back after the lecture, I will add this.—As we make our farewells let us say to ourselves that we will be true anthroposophists by remaining together in our souls through the spirit which becomes alive in us through our view of life. Let those of us who are now going away again say to our friends of the Breslau Group: we too will think about what we have been able to acquire for our own souls and those of others while working together with you. We will feel that we are with you even when we have gone away from this room and we hope that the Breslau friends too will think of those who were so glad to have been among them at this time.

# *Publisher's Note Regarding Rudolf Steiner's Lectures*

The lectures contained in this volume have been translated from the German which is based on stenographic and other recorded texts that were in most cases never seen or revised by the lecturer. Hence, due to human errors in hearing and transcription, they may contain mistakes and faulty passages. Every effort has been made to ensure that this is not the case. Some of the lectures were given to audiences more familiar with anthroposophy; these are the so-called 'private' or 'members' lectures. Other lectures, like the written works, were intended for the general public. The differences between these, as Rudolf Steiner indicates in his *Autobiography*, is twofold. On the one hand, the members' lectures take for granted a background in and commitment to anthroposophy; in the public lectures this was not the case. At the same time, the members' lectures address the concerns and dilemmas of the members, while the public work speaks directly out of Steiner's own understanding of universal needs. Nevertheless, as Rudolf Steiner stresses: 'Nothing was ever said that was not solely the result of my direct experience of the growing content of anthroposophy. There was never any question of concessions to the prejudices and preferences of the members. Whoever reads these privately printed lectures can take them to represent anthroposophy in the fullest sense. Thus it was possible without hesitation—when the complaints in this direction became too persistent—to depart from the custom of circulating this material "for members only". But it must be borne in mind that faulty passages do occur in these reports not revised by myself.' Earlier in the same chapter, he states: 'Had I been able to correct them [the private lectures] the restriction [for members only] would have been unnecessary from the beginning.'

## Karmic Relationships
Esoteric Studies

*The full series, now available:*

**Volume 1**
Features an overview of the laws and conditions of karma, and goes on to consider the incarnations of Friedrich Nietzsche, Lord Bacon of Verulam, Lord Byron and many others.
*Trans: G. Adams, rev. M. Cotterell, C. Davy & D. S. Osmond (12 lectures, Dornach, 16 Feb–23 Mar 1924, GA 235); 206pp; ISBN 0 85440 260 8*

**Volume 2**
Features individual karmic relationships in history—for example Marx and Engels—as well as a survey of karma in human life, the shaping of karma after death, and the 'cosmic form' of karma.
*Trans: G. Adams, rev. M. Cotterell, C. Davy & D. S. Osmond (16 lectures, Dornach, 6 Apr–29 Jun 1924, GA 236); 256pp; ISBN 0 85440 281 0*

**Volume 3**
The Karmic Relationships of the Anthroposophical Movement. Includes predispositions which lead souls to anthroposophy, the two streams within the movement, plus Rosicrucianism, Arabism, Aristotelianism, the Platonists and the School of Michael.
*Trans: G. Adams, rev. D. S. Osmond (11 lectures, Dornach, 1 Jul to 8 Aug 1924, GA 237); 180pp; ISBN 0 85440 313 2*

**Volume 4**
The karmic groups of souls connected to Aristotelianism and Platonism, the karma of the anthroposophical movement, as well as the individual incarnations of Ernst Haeckel, Vladimir Solovioff and others. This new edition also includes Steiner's last address.
*Trans: G. Adams, C. Davy & D. S. Osmond (11 lectures, Dornach, 5–24 Sept 1924, GA 238); 174pp; ISBN 0 85440 412 0*

**Volume 5**

The difference between 'moon karma' and 'sun karma', the influences of Christian and Mohammedan thinking, the transformation of inner human qualities from one life to the next, and much more.

*Trans: D. S. Osmond (7 lectures, Prague & Paris, 29 Mar–25 May 1924, GA 239); 112pp; ISBN 0 85440 432 5*

**Volume 6**

A study of the karma of the anthroposophical movement and society, the spiritual gates of the sun and moon, and much more.

*Trans: D. S. Osmond (9 lectures, various cities, 25 Jan–20 Jul 1924, GA 235, 236, 240); 184pp; ISBN 0 85440 242 X*

**Volume 7**

Human experiences after death and before a new birth; karma in world history; the cosmic nature of Christ; waking, dreaming, sleeping; the physical effects of karma, etc.

*Trans: D. S. Osmond (9 lectures, Breslau, 7–15 Jun 1924, GA 239); 144pp; ISBN 0 85440 276 4*

**Volume 8**

Subjects include Cosmic Christianity, the Michael impulse, the Arthur and Grail streams of wisdom, plus Gregory VII, Haeckel, Swedenborg, Loyola, Haroun al Raschid, Byron, Voltaire and others.

*Trans: D. S. Osmond (6 lectures, Torquay 12–21 Aug, London 24–27Aug 1924, GA 240); 102pp; ISBN 0 85440 018 4*